# ADVENTURES IN NICARAGUA:

## *Learning a culture piece by piece*

Ann Coyne

Copyright © 2024 Ann Coyne

All rights reserved.

# Contents

Foreword ................................................................. i
Chapter 1: Human Shields ............................................ 1
Chapter 2: Poverty .................................................... 22
Chapter 3: Dr. Roberto Calderon ................................. 49
Chapter 4: Sabbatical ................................................ 65
Chapter 5: Getting a Visa ........................................... 85
Chapter 6: Finding a Project ..................................... 101
Chapter 7: Semana Santa ......................................... 116
Chapter 8: Transfer of Power .................................... 130
Chapter 9: David ..................................................... 140
Chapter 10: International Adoption ........................... 161
Chapter 11: Snow White .......................................... 185
Acknowledgements ................................................. 201
Author Bio ............................................................. 202

# Foreword

How have I gotten myself into so many problems and so many adventures in Nicaragua, a tiny country in Central America? I had never set out to go there. I wasn't trying to save the world. Although I was a social work professor specializing in child welfare, I had never intended to do international adoptions or global social work. I was just going along with my friend Suzy on a little one-time adventure. It was a bit of a lark. When this 34-year-long Nicaraguan adventure started in 1984, I didn't even know how to speak Spanish.

# Chapter 1

# Human Shields

"You can't go, you'll be killed!" Jim shouted as he stomped out of the room and down the stairs. I was headed to Nicaragua with Witness for Peace in April 1984, and my 21-year-old son was not taking the news well. I was going with my friend, Suzy Prenger, into a war zone with the hope that the Contras would leave any area where American citizens were located. Essentially, we were to serve as human shields to protect the local people.

"She'll be fine," my husband, Dermot, yelled after him. "Your mother grew up in a big city; she won't do anything stupid." I expected Jim's outburst, but Dermot's vote of confidence in my survival instincts was a pleasant surprise. He'd done agricultural research in the Dominican Republic which required protection by an armed guard at night. He knew international work could be dangerous, but he trusted my big-city Boston instincts and good sense, and was resigned, if not enthused, about my trip. Plus, no Witness for Peace volunteer had ever been injured, as far as he, or I, knew.

Dermot, at 55, looked the same as he had at 25 when he first came to the U.S. from Ireland as an international graduate student in agriculture. We met as students at Cornell and married in 1957.

Because he had been admitted into the U.S. on a J1 Visa, we had only 30 days to leave the United States after he graduated, and he couldn't apply to return for two years. We lived in

England for two years and returned to the US in 1960 for him to look for a university position as a plant breeder.

After Jim made such a ruckus about my going to Nicaragua with Suzy, the two youngest of our six children, Cathy and Gerry, began paying attention. When they heard, "Witness for Peace instructs us to be sure our wills are up to date," both children whipped around, turning their backs on the TV to pay closer attention to the family drama. What was their mother up to now? She had taken them to the Capitol many times to demonstrate against the Vietnam War, but this seemed different.

My friend, Suzy Prenger, was also our Spanish instructor. Dermot's federal grant for developing disease resistant beans in the Dominican Republic also included funds for language training. To encourage the scientists working on the grant to speak Spanish at home, spouses were invited to also take the Spanish classes.

Suzy was in her 30s and studying for a doctorate in education. Although a native Nebraskan, she had lived in Spain for a year as an undergraduate and spoke Spanish fluently. At 5'5", she was a bit taller and heavier than me, with dark brown eyes and dark curly hair that was thick and tended to fly out of control. Whenever I saw her, she was always dressed in sensible clothes and sensible shoes. I don't think I ever saw her wearing makeup, high heels, or a fancy dress.

Her energy level was even higher than mine. During Spanish class, she bounded around the room full of good cheer, encouraging us all to try. Outside of class, she was always funny, outgoing, and in the center of a gaggle of people.

Looking at my worried children, I wondered, am I being crazy? I've always liked adventure and taking risks, but is this a bit too far? Suzy wouldn't take us into real danger... but if she did, I'd know enough not to stick around if I smelled trouble... I'm sure I'll be fine... anyway, I can always back out if I think the trip's too dangerous... I'll be fine... the kids are worrying too much... Dermot thinks it's ok...

Not long after President Reagan came to power in 1981, the U.S. began funding contra-revolutionary efforts in Nicaragua by members of the previous dictator's army, the Guardia Nacional, who had fled to Honduras after the triumph of the Sandinista Revolution in July 1979. The support by the U.S government of these mercenaries, commonly called the Contras, caught the attention of various peace activists in the U.S., including members of Nebraskans for Peace.

Those of us who had demonstrated during the Civil Rights era of the 1960s and the Vietnam Conflict of the 1970s found ourselves in the 1980s faced with a U.S. government, as part of its Cold War efforts, intent on propping up the right-wing governments in El Salvador and Guatemala and overthrowing the left-wing government in Nicaragua, which had aligned itself with Cuba, Russia, and the entire Eastern Block.

The U.S. government did not want the Central American countries in its backyard aligned with the Soviet Union, and invoked the Monroe Doctrine to justify its actions of funding a militia to overthrow the Sandinista Government. The Monroe Doctrine, established by President James Monroe in 1823, created separate spheres of European and American influence. It declared the U.S. would not tolerate intervention by European nations in the affairs of nations in the Western Hemisphere.

It was in this political context that my longtime friend and Spanish instructor, Suzy Prenger, agreed to lead a Nebraska/Kansas Witness-for-Peace delegation to Nicaragua in April 1984. One day in Spanish class, out of the blue, Suzy had asked me to come along with her to Nicaragua in April to oversee the health of the delegation she was leading. There were no doctors or nurses going, and I was the only one she knew who had any experience with hospitals. Unfortunately, my experience was limited to working as a nurse's aide in college and accompanying my six children to various emergency rooms. My meager medical knowledge could be contained in a Red Cross First Aid handbook.

I had seen the U.S. medical system in a full-court press when my son Tom was treated for, and survived, cancer in 1981, but I realized then that my medical knowledge was miniscule compared to those oncology doctors and nurses. Can I do this? I wondered. What if someone gets hurt or sick? What if someone dies? Do I have the experience to know what to do?

I began to feel very anxious about accepting this amount of responsibility for other people's lives. You can do this, I told myself. You are good in an emergency… you don't panic… However, I remained nervous and doubtful, wondering, will there be armed military men patrolling the streets and armed guards everywhere we go?

At age 48, I had lived through a lot of life experiences plus twenty years' activities as a child welfare advocate. In the process of adopting Cathy from the Department of Public Welfare, I realized how crazy the child welfare system was and how older or disabled children who needed to be adopted were essentially trapped by the bureaucracy. Thinking I could make a difference, I studied for a Masters in Social Work and a PhD in Management at the University of Nebraska. Before retiring in 2018, I had been a faculty member at the Grace Abbott School of Social Work at the University of Nebraska Omaha for 43 years. I spent 1981-1983 on loan to the State of Nebraska as Deputy Director of the State Department of Public Welfare (now called the Department of Health and Human Service).

But by 1984, Suzy knew I was back teaching at the university, rested enough from the stress of administering a $150 million budget, and looking for something different and interesting to do. She also knew me well enough to know I don't frighten easily, stay calm in a crisis, and would be able to establish control if anything unforeseen happened. I hoped she was right.

I had taken charge back in college when candles set the sheets on fire, that had been draped around the chapter room in the basement of my sorority house. When 40 fellow students, wrapped in togas, began screaming and running in circles, I hopped up on a chair and firmly started shouting "Everyone out… Everyone out." Like lemmings they followed my orders and the room was cleared before all the sheets lining the walls burst into flames. It was only after we were all safe upstairs that I felt the panic. At the time of the fire, I just switched into thinking mode, shut off the fear, and acted. Later this coping mechanism would come to my aid many times, for example when the Big Wheel sliced off Gerry's toe, when a student in scuba diving class sunk to the bottom of the pool, and the many times my children were sick or injured. My ability to shut down emotions and cope with the problem at hand has served me well in crises all my life. It is only after the crisis is over that I feel the fear and become emotional.

This trip might be interesting, I had thought, and, on a whim, agreed to go with Suzy as her health and safety aide, praying fervently that no one got sick or injured in Nicaragua.

Before we left, I visited individually with everyone traveling, reminded them to bring all their medicines, talked with a nursing professor that I knew, and debated buying the book, Where There is No Doctor, but could find only the Spanish version of it at the local Borders Book Store (there was no Amazon then for purchasing books over the internet, as there was no internet).

Joyce McPherson, one of the travelers going with us, worried me the most when I interviewed her about her health. Although she looked like a tall, healthy, 50-year-old woman with salt and pepper hair, Joyce had had surgery to have part of her intestine removed three weeks previously, and her doctor advised her not to go on the trip. When I tried to ask her about her health situation, she angrily told me, "I don't care what he says. I'm going. He told me if I went I had to bring all my food with me, so I packed two weeks' worth of things I can eat that don't need to be refrigerated." I was not reassured.

Our Witness-for-Peace delegation was a motley crew of fourteen aging civil rights and anti-war activists from the 1960s.

One man, Henry Sorensen, was in his late 70s and had been involved in antiwar activities at the end of the 1930s, a time when most of the U.S. population believed in isolation from Europe's wars. The two Catholic priests were in their 40s and had been very active in civil rights marches in the 1960s. The two Mennonite farmers were in their 50s, as was the wife of the sitting Republican Governor of Nebraska, Charlie Thone. Ruth Thone was not on the same page, or even in the same book, as her husband politically.

While the Governor was President Reagan's reelection campaign chair in Nebraska in 1984, his wife Ruth was demonstrating with us in front of the U.S. Embassy in Managua against Reagan's Nicaraguan policies.

Although Ruth and Joyce were best friends, they looked very different. Ruth was a bit over-weight and short, about my height of 5'2", while Joyce was thin and tall at 5'10." Always together, they looked like Mutt and Jeff (the odd-couple in the long running comic strip in every Sunday newspaper at the time).

After an emotional send off the night before our trip, by a group from Nebraskans for Peace at St. Timothy's Church in Omaha, we left on a Delta Airlines plane for Atlanta where we would board the flight to Managua. When we arrived at the gate in Atlanta for international departures, we noticed people gathered in large groups, wearing different colored t-shirts with Spanish words as they waited for the Managua plane. The green ones, worn by 10-15 strong looking men in their 30s and 40s, read "Plumbers for Nicaragua." The red t-shirts stated "Medical Mission for Nicaragua," and were worn by older men and women who looked more like doctors and nurses than revolutionaries. The blue t-shirts proclaimed "God loves Nicaragua." People wearing the blue t-shirts were the most numerous. Those travelers ranged from teenagers with mothers and fathers in tow, to older men with the look of Protestant Ministers.

When I talked to one of the women, I could hear her strong southern accent. They were from a Southern Baptist congregation in Alabama, and were going to a small town south of Managua to build a church. I have mixed feelings about missionary work. It makes me nervous that people may base their help on the recipient's willingness to convert.

As I would later learn, evangelical missionaries provide a lot of help to impoverished Nicaraguans, as well as converting them from Catholicism to evangelical Christianity. I have negative feelings about mission work that focuses on converting people away from their own religion, probably based on my Irish background where, during the famine in the 1840s, Protestants withheld food from starving Irish peasants if they wouldn't deny Catholicism, "take the soup," and become Protestants. On the other hand, I have strong positive feelings for the many Southern Baptists from the U.S. that spend time and Treasure making sure Nicaraguan children are fed and housed. Couldn't you just feed and care for them, without trying to convert them? I wonder silently.

When we arrived in Managua we had to walk down the stairs of the plane and across the tarmac. The hot air rushing over us made me feel like I was descending into an oven. After we exited from immigration and customs, we spotted a Witness for Peace sign held high by two long-term volunteers. Jennifer Coleman and Nancy Sullivan led us out of the airport and toward an old green bus that had seen better days.

In Nicaragua, we were transported in the old, square, 20-passenger bus that started only when people got behind it and pushed it downhill. Often, it belched black smoke over those pushing when it jumped into gear, and the motor started with a bang.

It looked like it might have been a school bus at one point, but it had been heavily used and repainted green with a white stripe, though most of that paint was flaking off. Inside, the brown imitation leather seat covers were ripped, and the fold-down jump seats were without padding. The cover for the ceiling inside the bus was missing, exposing rusted studs supporting the metal roof. The bus had seen better days, but it ran well enough to take us where we needed to go.

The bus driver, Alvaro Mejia, was a middle-aged Nicaraguan who lived in Managua and worked for Witness for Peace. He was about 40 years old, short like most Nicaraguan men, although at 5'4" he was taller than me. His skin was dark brown, and because he was out in the sun so much, he had a farmer's tan on his left arm that rested on the open window when he drove. His straight black hair was cut short and was beginning to recede in the front. Alvaro never said much, even to Suzy or the long-term Witness for Peace volunteers. He listened to the radio and drove.

And what a ride! Most of the roads were filled with potholes, so we bounced along in the old bus, which was missing shock absorbers as well as paint. Since March and April, the hottest months, are in the dry season, the air was full of dust that blew across the empty fields, through the open windows of the bus, and landed on our sweaty faces, emphasizing every wrinkle.

All of us stayed together in a Mennonite-run hostel, a large house called La Quinta, rented by Witness for Peace for the short-term delegations that came from the U.S. every two weeks. La Quinta was located on the western edge of Managua at the foot of an inactive volcano with enormous letters, FSLN (Frente Sandinista de la Liberación de Nicaragua i.e., the Sandinistas) mounted on its side, like the Hollywood letters on the side of a hill in California. There was no danger of our driver getting lost when looking for the hostel, as the volcano and its letters were visible all over Managua. The sight of the letters was comforting, as I felt there was no way to get lost, even in a city of over one million people.

The hostel was shaded by many tall trees and bushes and had two large dorms, one for men and another for women, plus a large kitchen, living room, and eating area. The two dorms had seven metal bunk beds, so they could sleep 14 people each. Fortunately, we had few enough people that we could all sleep on bottom bunks.

The bathrooms were dormitory style with metal stalls. The showers had no shower curtains, the toilets no seats, and, as we had been warned, there was no toilet paper. People with camping experience laughed at our shock at the toilets. Suzy told us, "Just sit on the edge of the toilet, but be careful not to fall in." She also suggested that we carry our rolls of toilet paper with us wherever we went, along with our little bottles of hand sanitizer.

A bigger surprise was that the shower had only one faucet, marked F (Frio i.e., cold). There was no hot water anywhere in the country apparently. The knowledge that we had no hot water for showers brought the tour of the female facilities to a standstill. "How do we take a shower?" Joyce asked, still clutching her two-week supply of food.

"With cold water," Suzy announced with a laugh. For a group of women that were seemingly unconcerned about being in a war zone, the absence of hot water caused an unexpected sense of danger… even more than the danger of falling, bottom first, into the toilet.

Oh Lord, I thought. Showering is going to be like swimming in the cold Atlantic Ocean. I remember the drill. Splash some cold water on your arms and legs… first put one whole arm in followed by the other… then hold your breath and dunk your whole self quickly. I hated it as a child. But I also remembered that once I got fully in the water, it didn't seem so cold. Don't be a sissy! I told myself. If Suzy can do this, so can you.

The floors in the entire house were made of 12-inch square off-white tiles, which the maid mopped constantly, when she was not helping the cook chop up vegetables in the kitchen. She never sat down to rest. I realized that while she worked hard all day, she undoubtedly was being paid only a few Córdobas. I felt sad that she had to work so hard for so little, and angry that life was grossly unfair. In the U.S., we bitch and moan about having so much to do, I thought. We'd drop over dead if we had to work this hard.

The furniture in the large living room was made entirely of wood. There was a wooden couch with a rattan seat and spindle back that seated three. All the other seating involved a dozen or more wooden rocking chairs, called colloquially sillas abuelitas (literally, grandmother chairs), and large floor cushions of red, green, blue, and yellow. Most of the rocking chairs were made of light brown wood, probably pine, with woven rattan backs and seats, but a few were constructed of dark wood, possibly mahogany. Rectangular mats hung on the walls… volcanoes, fish, women with baskets on their heads, or pre-Colombian designs, woven in jute which had been dyed in red, blue, green, black and yellow colors. Two of the mats appeared to be fading from the bright sunlight that covered them in the morning. One large 5' by 5' square mat, depicting a woman with a long black braid down her back and a basket of vegetables on her head, was stretched from its own weight and was no longer square.

The dining room was furnished with what looked like light brown wooden picnic tables. There was enough table space for 28 visitors, but we needed only half the tables.

It was like a glass half-full with all the extra room. The kitchen was large, but surprisingly there was no oven; there was only a two-burner stove top, like ones used for camping. Two large pans were simmering rice on it, while the cook cut bananas and other colorful but unfamiliar fruits at the central work area. The whole room had a slight smell of cilantro.

Before dinner, several of us wandered outside. On the major highway in front of the hostel, in addition to the cars and trucks whizzing by, a wooden cart drawn by two oxen lumbered along carrying 12-foot-long pieces of wood, which I assumed were building materials.

On the sidewalk, a young boy about 10, barefoot and dressed only in jeans, pushed his younger sister in a homemade wooden cart with wooden wheels. Those of us with cameras motioned to him indicating, "Can we take your picture?" He understood our gestures, smiled and stood with his hands on his hips trying to look cool. His little sister, a bit afraid of us, ducked down and peered over the side of the wooden cart, only her eyes and dark curly hair visible.

After the sun set and we were getting ready for bed, I noticed that Mary Ann Singleton was missing. She was only 25 years old and had left a 9-month-old baby at home. At 5'2" and still a little plump around the middle, carrying the 'baby fat' she had not yet lost, Mary Ann had dark-brown shoulder-length hair and a pretty round face. As the women continued to laugh and joke about whether they would dare to take a cold shower tonight or wait until the morning, I started looking around the women's dorm.

"Has anyone seen Mary Ann?" I asked. Suddenly I spotted her standing in a dark corner crying silently and shaking like a leaf. I ran over and asked, "What's wrong?"

No answer. "Are you scared?" Nothing. "Are you missing your baby?" Still no answer. She just stood there shaking. For what seemed like an eternity she didn't speak, but then said, "Sometimes I get anxiety attacks." I pressed her further. "I've had to go to the hospital a couple of times," she whimpered.

Oh damn! I thought.

"Go over to the men's dormitory and find Larry Zink," I begged Joyce who was standing nearby. "Tell him I need him here right away." I flashed back to when I worked as a nurse's aide in college. I remembered a young mother who came into the hospital several time with her arms paralyzed from an anxiety attack. She would sit in the hospital bed for several days, and we would have to feed her, since she couldn't move either arm. She couldn't walk very well either. She was paralyzed by anxiety.

Oh my God. How am I going to cope with this? I thought, trying to remain calm. I looked around the women's dorm; none of the other women appeared to know what to do either. We are in a foreign country. We don't speak the language. It is possible Mary Ann may need to be hospitalized, for a mental health issue, for God's sake, in a country which probably doesn't have mental health treatment except in a locked mental institution for chronic patients. My stomach tightened as I remembered that I was the one who was supposed to deal with medical issues. I hadn't expected a mental health crisis, and I had no clue what had triggered Mary Ann's anxiety attack.

I told myself, take control… think… you're a social worker. But then I remembered, not that kind of social worker… you do policy and administration, not mental health… Fighting my panic, I told myself keep calm… all problems can be solved… but I was not totally convinced.

"If anyone knows what to do, it is Larry," I whispered to Suzy, who by then was standing next to me, equally concerned.

"Larry was a conscientious objector during the Vietnam War," I reminded her. "He was either a medic or a prisoner. Either way, he's sure to know what to do."

Larry appeared in the women's dorm, and I was jarringly reminded that at 6'4" and well under 200 pounds, he was unusually tall and thin. In the dark he looked a bit like a scarecrow. He had light brown thinning and receding hair, and a little mustache. Although he was a friend of my son Brian, he was quite a bit older than him. He wrapped his long arms around the shaking young woman and kept telling her, "You're Okay, Mary Ann! You're Okay!" It seemed to work. Within minutes she seemed to absorb his calm. He stood there holding her until the shaking stopped. Calmed down, she fell into bed and drifted off to sleep. The rest of the women followed suit, electing to put off their cold showers until morning. Peace descended on the women's dorm.

As the other women fell asleep, I lay awake worrying about Mary Ann. What have I gotten myself into? What if she has another anxiety attack? What if Larry can't settle her down? I had visions of us admitting her to a hospital where no one spoke English, or, more likely, one of us, probably me, having to change our tickets and take her back to Omaha. I know no one dies of an anxiety attack, but we won't be able to take her with us in a paralyzed state, I thought. Then it hit me. How will I take her on a plane if she is paralyzed? I could hear the deep breathing of the other women in the dorm; two were already snoring.

I stared at the tin roof over our heads which was visible in the pale-yellow light coming in the large unshaded dormitory window from a distant streetlight. Maybe if I count the cross beams, I will fall asleep. I counted them, but then my Freshman year engineering training kicked in and I found myself trying to figure out how the building was constructed. This is not helping me fall asleep, I whimpered. But I was so tired from the flight and the temperature change, from the low 30s when we left Omaha that morning to the high 90s now, that I eventually dropped off despite my runaway thoughts.

Sunrise comes early in the tropics. Even in a city of over a million people, all the roosters were up greeting the sun and making a racket by 5 a.m., accompanied by barking dogs and fruit and vegetable vendors walking along the streets with enormous baskets on their heads shouting, "mangos! papas! remolachas…"

As we gathered in the dining room for a breakfast of rice and beans, I discovered that the night had not passed so peacefully in the men's dorm. Dennis asked us, "Did you hear the shelling last night?"

The women, who had slept soundly, were mystified. "No. no. We didn't hear anything," said Ruth.

Dennis informed us that they were awakened by strange loud noises, like shells being lobbed onto the tin roof of the house. He told us that as soon as Fred heard the first noise, he started yelling, "Wake up! We are being shelled!" and ordered the others into a defensive alignment. "Spread out! Dale, you get over there to guard that side. Jack, you go over there by the window. If an attack comes, we need to be ready to defend our group."

Henry chimed in, "All night long the shelling continued, Boom… Boom Boom… Boom. But no soldiers showed up."

Suzy got the attention of the maid while all of us watched, now totally awake and focused. Suzy pointed excitedly to the roof and asked in Spanish, "Who was bombing us last night?"

The maid seemed confused. She looked at the roof where Suzy was pointing and then at the 14 sets of worried eyes staring intently at her. Slowly a smile spread over her face and she broke into a laugh. Her words came tumbling out, with Suzy's translation barely keeping up, "No one was shelling you. Those are mangos, not bombs, hitting the tin roof!"

We all rushed outside to inspect the offending tree, which hovered 30 feet over the men's wing of the house with hundreds of ripe mangos ready to fall. Sheepishly we crept back into the house to finish eating our breakfasts and prepare for our first day of being human shields.

At that point I was certain we were in over our heads… way over our heads. We didn't know the language or anything about the culture or even about the fruit trees. Who knew that mangos fell on the roofs of houses… or that people built houses under mango trees… or that mango trees were so common and so tall? Maybe this trip isn't such a good idea after all. But here we are… there is no way to go but forward… Soon after breakfast on the fourth day, after spending many hot days in Managua sitting on metal folding chairs in crowded offices, listening to translated information about the Sandinista Revolution, Sheila Shaw, a Witness-for-Peace long-term volunteer, told us that we would not be going north. We were originally supposed to go to Leon and then head north to the front, to Jalapa or Ocotal near the Honduran border where Nicaraguan farmers were being killed by the Contras. But a couple of weeks earlier the Witness for Peace South Dakota delegation had gone north, and a truck driving behind them hit a land mine. No one in the South Dakota delegation was injured, but we were not going north. It was too dangerous; the road was mined. Still upset over the South Dakota incident, the long-term volunteers were undecided about what to do with us before they took us to Potosi during the second week of the trip.

"Maybe we'll take you to the beach when we get to Leon," Sheila suggested.

"No, we want to do something to help, not go to the beach like a bunch of tourists," Rick argued, to cheers from the group. "There must be something we can do."

We bumped along all afternoon heading north from Managua to Leon, hitting potholes every few minutes or swerving to avoid one. People who had managed to fall asleep would wake with a start when we hit a large pothole and the entire bus shivered with the shock of the bump. Sleepers would open their eyes in fear, but then fall back to sleep. I was more interested in viewing the countryside than sleeping.

The land was very dry with gusts of wind swirling small clumps of top soil into the air like mini tornados. What type of crops do they grow here? I wondered, observing a few dead plants. This land is flat, and except for the volcanos, looks a lot like Nebraska. I'll bet they can grow crops here, although irrigation may be a problem. I looked around the fields to see if there was any indication of irrigation pipe or center pivot irrigation. Nothing. Just swirling dust rising into the air.

In the distance, I could see a few animals. Several oxen looked healthy, but the cattle looked as if they were dying. Their skin hung loosely over their bones, every one of which was visible. They looked more like skeletons than like cows. One of the farmers with us was awake.

"Josh, why do the cows look so bad?" I asked. "Are they starving?"

"Yes, they don't have nearly enough to eat," he replied. "But they also have intestinal parasites. They need more food, but it won't do them much good if they don't have treatment for parasites by a veterinarian." I am always amazed at how much farmers can tell about the land and about the animals just by looking.

After we arrived in Leon, we had a pot luck dinner in one of the houses where we would be staying in Fundesi, a neighborhood near the Medical Campus in Leon. Women from each of the 14 families who were hosting us brought typical Nicaraguan food which we ate sitting on the floor or on chairs, wherever we could find a spot.

The mixture of beans and rice, called gallopinto, was a favorite of everybody.

Some people were afraid to eat the salad, because they couldn't peel the vegetables, as suggested in the How to Stay Safe on Your Trip brochure. I was less concerned and ate the salad as well as the tasty fried chicken. After dinner, we all walked home with our assigned families along dusty dirt paths to the houses where we would be staying.

My family consisted of Fernando, his wife Eugenia, plus their teenage daughter, Karla, who had a 6-month-old baby, Cristina. Fernando was very friendly and told me he worked at the Dental School, a short walk away from Fundesi, on the Medical campus. As we sat at the kitchen table, he tried to explain to me, very slowly and with lots of hand motions so I might understand, all the changes that had taken place in Nicaragua since the Sandinista Revolution was successful, five years before in 1979. President Somoza had been defeated, and the Sandinista party had taken over the government and was implementing many changes.

"They want women to be equal," he told me, looking not fully convinced. "I try, but it is hard," he laughed, looking over at Eugenia, who rolled her eyes.

That night I slept on a straw-filled mattress that was laid over strips of heavy cloth stretched tight across a wooden bedstead. When I got into bed, I sunk into the mattress, hoping it wouldn't fall through the strips of cloth and land me on the floor. Sharp pieces of straw stuck into my legs, my back, my neck.

There must be a way to make this more comfortable, I thought, as I punched the straw so I could lay my head on it. I hope this mattress doesn't poke me all night.

I liked being with a family. It is nice to meet real Nicaraguans, I thought, even though I can't understand much of what they are saying. Fernando is trying so hard to be friendly. Someday my Spanish will be better, I promised myself, as I drifted off to sleep on my lumpy bed of straw.

In the morning after breakfast, the long-term volunteers announced they had found a job for us, and we prepared to go to a cotton field on the outskirts of Leon; it had been harvested a few days before, and we were to pick what the harvesters missed. Everyone gathered at the Maryknoll House, walking from the nearby houses where we had slept. Suzy told us to be sure to bring our hats and lots of sunscreen to shade ourselves against the blazing sun bearing down from high overhead in a cloudless sky.

"Make sure you have your two-liter water bottles with you," Suzy reminded the group as we gathered in the yard. She and I checked that each person had enough water and a hat.

Jennifer, one of the long-term Witness for Peace volunteers shouted, "Okay guys, Alvaro needs a push to get the bus started. Then we'll head for the field to pick cotton."

Mary Ann and Suzy joined Jennifer and the men behind the bus, pushing it 50 yards or more down the slight incline in front of the Maryknoll House.

They huffed and strained as they pushed, sweat dripping off their faces and feet slipping on the soft dust of the road. This was not an easy job. The other older women and I watched in amusement as the bus lunged and lurched along the nearly flat street, pushed by people running at full speed, sometimes slipping and dropping back, unable to catch up again with the rapidly accelerating bus. Alvaro shoved it into gear, and the old bus jumped like it had hit a wall. Bang! The metal screeched. Whoosh! Black smoke billowed out the tailpipe. The shaking bus took a couple of gasps then settled down to a loud hum. We were ready. It did occur to me as I watched the effort it took to push it up to speed, that someday the bus might not start, stranding us in an out-of-the-way spot. But I had enough things to worry about, that I decided not to worry about something that had not yet happened.

While the group went to the field with burlap sacks to help with the cotton harvest, Sister Rita, a tough little Maryknoll nun of 60, who grew up on the streets of Chicago, drove me, sweating like a pig because it was nearly 90 degrees, in her little Volkswagen Bug to the telephone company in Leon to file a story with the Lincoln Journal, the daily evening paper in Lincoln, Nebraska.

The editor was very interested in what Ruth Thone, Nebraska's First Lady, was up to in Nicaragua. I could barely hear the reporter's questions, but I shouted into the phone "We are in Leon picking cotton today! Tomorrow we go to Potosi on the Gulf of Fonseca where the US Central Intelligence Agency boats shelled the port and destroyed the Customs House!"

All the people in the large room, which had 10 or more black phones hanging out of the white painted walls at head height, stopped their phone calls and turned around to watch me yell unintelligible English words into my phone, with Sister Rita, shorter than me, and as round as she was tall, correcting the spelling of the place names.

Returning to the car, we walked past some of the buildings of the National University, UNAN-Leon, which were covered with colorful political graffiti such as: No Pasaran (they will not pass) and, in relation to the university, 6% Para la Universidad, the percentage of national funding the universities were supposed to get (but never did). Students lounged on the steps of the chemistry building drinking a red liquid out of plastic bags. It was Rosita, a cold sugary soft drink that was less expensive than Coke or Pepsi. We watched as the drink vendor poured a bottle of Rosita into a plastic bag and flung the bag in an arc around his hand to make a knot. A student took the bag and held it above his face, took a bite out of a corner, and sucked it down. Some students, and Sister Rita, held the bag especially high, and let the liquid pour as a stream into their mouths. I tried it and spilled red Rosita down the front of my white blouse. It wasn't as easy as it looked!

The vendor did not allow anyone to touch the glass bottles, because the next day he could refill and sell only the number of bottles he had returned to the processing plant that day. Poverty displayed itself in various ways in this poorest of all countries in the Western Hemisphere. Even Haiti was doing a little better economically in 1984.

Sucking on our plastic bags of Rosita, we found the car and headed for the cotton field on the outskirts of Leon where the others were harvesting cotton. As soon as Sister Rita and I stepped out of the car, I smelled danger. There was a unique scent in the air that I had smelled once before, when we tried to enter one of Dermot's greenhouses on the agricultural campus of the university in Lincoln.

"What is that awful smell?" I had asked Dermot as soon as he opened the greenhouse door, realizing I had never smelled anything like it before.

"Parathion," he shouted, as he quickly shut the door of the greenhouse. He was angry. "Some graduate student fumigated the greenhouse and didn't put the Keep-Out sign on the door. Parathion is a very dangerous insecticide. It can be absorbed through the skin. If you ever smell anything like this again, stay away from it. It could kill you," he warned as he tried to figure out in his mind which graduate student was going to hear from him about this serious error.

As we got out of the car, I yelled at Sister Rita, "I think this field may have been sprayed with parathion." Spotting a metal oil barrel about 50 feet away, I said, "Wait here, I am going to check," and ran over to a large open barrel filled to the brim with liquid. It was labeled "Parathion." I immediately started shouting, "Get out of the field! Get out of the field! It's been sprayed with parathion!" as I ran toward the group picking cotton. Dragging their half-full bags of cotton, people came toward the bus. I spotted Ruth who was waving her arms at the far edge of the cotton field.

When I got to her, she told me, "Something's wrong with Joyce, she doesn't know who she is or where she is."

We went straight back to the Maryknoll House. I ordered everyone to strip off their clothes, get into the showers, and scrub their skin thoroughly. "This stuff is poisonous and is easily absorbed through the skin!" I hollered after them as they headed for the showers wrapped only in towels. Joyce was in the worst shape, so I told the other women, "Wash yourselves, but be sure to wash Joyce too." By the time Ruth and I got her stripped of her clothes, Joyce was so confused that giving her directions was useless. Sister Rita and I then ran around picking up all the discarded clothing for the maid to wash, hoping to God we wouldn't poison her too.

After their showers the men seemed fine. But all the women, except Suzy and me, were sick. I placed blankets on the lawn for some to rest on and put Joyce and Ruth, who were the sickest, into beds.

After a three-hour nap, Joyce finally knew who and where she was. Ruth felt less sick, and the other women seemed fine. None of the seven men ever had signs of being poisoned. I kept trying to figure out the gender differences. Maybe it's body size, I theorized. But two of the men are small. Perhaps it is the higher fat content of women's bodies absorbing more of the poison… I wasn't sure. I was just glad that no one had to be hospitalized, especially in Nicaragua. I remembered the hospital we visited two days before in Managua where we donated all the medical supplies we had brought with us.

I couldn't imagine putting any of our group there, even though this hospital was supposed to be one of the best in the country, a 'hospital of reference' as it was called.

As we toured the facility I thought, this place is so filthy, if any of us become a patient here, we will pick up TB or some other infection. No way will I put anyone in here! None of the staff were wearing rubber gloves, not even when treating a patient with open wounds.

There was blood on the floor and bloody rags in the corner of rooms. Along the corridor in front of the public restroom, there was water and urine half-inch deep covering the floor, with large squares of cardboard placed here and there to soak it up. The smell of urine and methane was sickening. How do the patients, doctors, and nurses stand it? I thought.

Medical care and medical equipment in the hospital was primitive. I saw one patient who was receiving an IV; the bag was attached to the top of the handle of a yellow wooden broom. This gerrymandered contraption was then duct-taped to the metal springs and the metal side of the patient's bed. In addition to primitive medical equipment, all the doctors we saw in the hospital were very young. Most looked like they were medical students just out of high school. A few appeared to be 22 or 23. Please God, let us get home safely, I thought. I'm responsible for everyone's health, and there's no medical backup here. We are like the Pioneers going across the Great Plains in their covered wagons… on our own. The parathion incident was a close call. Our trip easily could have turned tragic. We badly needed an agricultural expert with us in a country that had no environmental controls. Additionally, we needed a doctor, or at least a nurse.

We certainly needed more than me. I couldn't even speak the language, let alone understand the environment we were in. But we had completed one week of the trip. One more week to go. Please God, no more problems.

# Chapter 2

# Poverty

The day following the poisoning in Leon we met with the Sandinista Army officer responsible for the northwest sector of the country. Sergio Parajon was 24 years old, the same age as my son Brian, and reminded me of him. He was taller than most Nicaraguan men, perhaps 5'7", slim with light brown skin and brown hair. He looked more like a Spaniard than a Nicaraguan and probably came from an upper-class family. He seemed very capable, despite his young age. Sergio's northwest sector included the main agricultural area of the country as well as the large Port of Corinto, which I subsequently found out was the busiest port south of Los Angeles. By the 2000s, it will move tons of cargo containers from all over the Pacific. But in 1984, the US Central Intelligence Agency (CIA) had mined the harbor, and the week before we came, a Russian fishing trawler hit a U.S. mine and sank.

Twenty-somethings were running the entire country. Sergio was 24, and the physician who was chief of staff at the hospital we visited in Managua was 25. We were all old enough to be their parents or grandparents.

Watching Suzy negotiate with Sergio, I wondered if she and the others were as nervous as I was about youngsters overseeing everything. This country is in the middle of a war. Do they know what they are doing?

Twenty-somethings running a country after a revolution is a phenomenon reminiscent of the Founding Fathers in the U.S. as well. Most of them were very young, except for Benjamin Franklin, who brought wisdom and experience to the younger ones like Alexander Hamilton or Sam Adams. Young people bring energy and new ideas to a new country, but they also have limited experience and make many mistakes. They have the greatest passion for changing the world, but often the least understanding of how to do it. I hope they don't get us into difficulty.

Sergio told us we could go to Chinandega and from there to Potosi, but we had to be accompanied by some soldiers. Our 'minder' was Carlos Hernandez, a young man with an AK-47, a kid really, about 19, the same age as my daughter and younger than my four oldest sons. The other soldier, Daniel Gonzalez, looked even younger, perhaps 17 or 18. It was like going on a trip with teenagers dressed up as soldiers. Both young men were no more than 5' 3", with dark skin. Daniel had straight black hair and looked a bit taller than Carlos because he was thinner. Carlos had black tight curly crispo hair, cut short in military style. They smiled a lot and kept up a series of stories about Nicaragua, despite our not understanding a word of what they were saying. Daniel was less chatty than Carlos and looked to him for information and direction. I'm not sure they ever caught on that we didn't understand them, because we smiled and nodded in agreement at everything they told us. We knew Suzy would fill us in later.

Carlos and Daniel were dressed in their khaki army uniforms, but like most Nicaraguans, male and female, they were very relaxed and friendly.

It was hot, so they unbuttoned the top two or three buttons of their uniform shirts, which were wrinkled and well lived in. They reminded me a bit of the East High School track team on their way to a meet, dressed in their old clothes, although Carlos was a bit overweight for a runner. I wondered if they had received any military training. They didn't act like the soldiers in Mexico, who are a bit full of themselves and imperious. They acted more like the 18-22 year-olds who hung out at my house and threw footballs to each other in the front yard. I liked our soldiers a lot and didn't have any worry that they would hurt us. I just wished I could understand their stories.

It was hot, the hottest month in Nicaragua, and everything looked dead. The land was bone dry, as the rains had not yet come. The trees stood like skeletons, brown and withered without leaves. There was no grass, just brown dust swirling across fields in small sandstorms. No birds or insects flew overhead, as the sun bore straight down on our heads from the blue cloudless sky. As we waited for security clearance at the road block on the outskirts of Leon, some of us sat on the brown dusty ground, trying to stay in the shade of the bus and amuse ourselves by chatting with Carlos.

A few of us women eyed the weapon, held upright in Carlos' left hand as he sat on the ground with us. We made gestures to see if he would show us how it worked. He laughed; middle-aged gringas, interested in a weapon. Eventually, he took it apart to show us how it fit together.

It seemed sturdy and rather easy to take apart and put back together. So, this is what an AK-47 looks like, I thought. I wonder if it's heavy. He didn't let us test that question. He held on tightly to his weapon. Look but don't touch, he seemed to indicate.

When Sergio finally gave us permission to travel, we and our AK-47 armed soldiers started out for Potosi in our rickety bus. After we got beyond Chinandega and headed north along the coast, we bumped along in the ancient bus over pot holes, searching the passing fields for anything alive or green. All we saw were leafless trees, swirling topsoil, starving animals, and scorching sunlight. Occasionally we would come upon a group of houses, each about 8' by 8' square, made of cardboard shipping containers.

Bouncing along, I hoped the rifles had sturdy safety locks on them, and we wouldn't have any further demonstration of their use. Maybe if I think of the rifles as decorations, I won't feel so uneasy sitting beside them, I thought. Carlos and Daniel seem like nice young men, I reassured myself. They are not going to shoot anyone. It was like my teenage kids were coming with us on a camping trip, except these teens had AK-47s and were dressed in Army fatigues.

We needed these soldiers for us to travel to Potosi, because to go anywhere in the conflict zone, we had to go through numerous checkpoints on the side of the road manned by the Army. Carlos showed the proper documents that gave us clearance, so the young men manning the checkpoints let us pass. Clearly this area of Nicaragua was under heavy military control, although we didn't see or hear any fighting.

When we got to Potosi, on the shore of the Gulf of Fonseca, we could see Honduras across the Gulf, where the U.S. had seven air force bases. "Is that El Salvador in the distance on the left?" I wondered out loud, trying to orient myself on my mental map of Central America. No one knew, including Carlos, Daniel, or our driver Alvaro. North Americans are not the only ones who have trouble with geography, I discovered.

There were only 40 people left living there in the little town of Potosi. It clearly had been a fishing village and a working port, with a customs house now standing in ruins from a CIA attack. I photographed it and imagined the customs house as a lovely red brick building, with many ships tied up at its pier, waiting to deliver cartons of building materials or food. But all that remained were parts of four brick walls and a pretty white door that opened into the empty space where customs officials used to clear materials in and out of Nicaragua. The top of the customs house was gone. Maybe it had a steeple that got blown off in the attack; I didn't know. It just seemed like it needed a steeple, like the customs house in Boston.

I looked around the remnants of the port. No fishing boats were visible anywhere in the Gulf. In fact, there was very little activity of any kind on the water, except for what might have been small military gunboats in the distance. Imagining what was, and looking now at the destruction in front of me, I felt sad for the Nicaraguans and at the same time, angry at the CIA, my own government, for damaging such a beautiful location. Later that day I would see the effects of their attacks on the people.

In Potosi, for the first time, we saw signs of malnutrition. Leaving Leon, we had stopped in Chinandega, the market town for the region where we saw lots of boys, perhaps 10-12 years old, with black hair and flat bellies, working in the market. They pushed carts around from stall to stall, loaded with 50-pound bags of dry beans or rice and 5-foot diameter wicker baskets filled with vegetables. Every child we saw there looked healthy and strong.

But at Potosi, especially among the younger children, we began to see signs of the protein missing from their diets. The babies still being nursed looked fine, but the toddlers displaced from their mother's breast by a younger sibling had the telltale yellow streaks of protein deficiency in their hair and the round bellies of malnutrition. Lack of protein in small children affects the development of their brains as well as their hair.

I picked up a little boy who had wandered away from his mother, sitting nearby, nursing a younger sister. He was tiny with very dark skin and jet black hair with streaks of yellow. When I asked him his name, he just smiled. A woman nearby said his name was "Enrique." When I asked how old he was though, he held up four fingers. I looked at the yellow streaks in four-year-old Enrique's hair that were screaming 'malnutrition' and wondered as I held him, what is going to become of this little boy? What have we done to him? Holding him protectively in my arms, I felt personably responsible for Enrique's situation. I sought to protect him, but knew that I couldn't. It is a miserable feeling to be powerless.

Although it was a fishing village, the boats were moored and the nets stored away. The residents told us the CIA had small gunboats in the Gulf of Fonseca that shelled anyone trying to fish. Clearly the attacks were designed to terrorize the population and convince them that the Sandinistas couldn't protect them. Maybe that is what those little boats in the distance are, I thought. CIA gunboats. Every time I hear the hymn in Spanish, "Pescadores de Almas" (Fishermen of Souls) I am transported back to Potosi and remember Enrique and the moored fishing boats, and his jet-black hair with streaks of yellow and wonder out loud to anyone who will listen, whatever did we think we were doing in Central America in the 1980s? Why were we torturing those people? What had they ever done to us?

There was a fresh water spring nearby that carried water from the mountains into a little river where the women were washing their clothes and swimming, fully clothed. We decided to join them, swimming in our clothes as well, because in the heat we knew we'd dry off in an hour or so. As I climbed fully clothed, but dripping wet, out of the river at Potosi, cool at last and free from the layer of dust that coated my hair, skin, and clothes, I laughed giddily about our dripping wet clothes, pleased and feeling a bit naughty, like an adolescent after skinny-dipping with friends.

As I looked up from drying my feet, one of the Nicaraguan women who had been with us in the water ran over to where I was drying off, dragging a small girl behind her. The woman was small, shorter than five feet, with dark brown skin and long black hair pulled back into a ponytail.

Her skinny arms and bony shoulders were visible under the wet dress clinging tightly to her body. Because of her many wrinkles, she looked as if she were 60-years-old, but she probably was under 40. The little girl, silent and petrified, stared glassy-eyed at me. She looked about eight or nine, and was as thin as her mother, her bones clearly visible under her wet clingy dress. Like her mother, she also had long black hair, but I noticed wisps of yellow among the black hairs when I looked closely.

The mother kept saying "mi hija" (my daughter) and "trece"

(13) plus many other words I didn't understand.

I kept repeating, "no comprendo, no comprendo" (I don't understand), but she continued to talk rapidly in Spanish, trying to convince me of something.

From her gestures and contorted face, I knew that she was terrified. She was not requesting money. She was begging for help, for safety, for something... but I couldn't figure out what. I felt totally useless. Why haven't I studied Spanish more? I thought, desperately trying to make sense of the woman's nonverbal gestures if not her words. Finally, I spotted Suzy in the river, and motioned for her to come translate.

The mother told us, "U.S. planes fly over every few days and make a big noise... but it is not a bomb."

I nodded my head and thought, oh wonderful, the U.S. Air Force pilots break the sound barrier as they exit Nicaragua and head out from Potosi over the Gulf of Fonseca to their bases in Honduras.

The mother continued, "We know it is not a bomb... we know they are trying to scare us... we're not scared..." But she looked terrified, sure that the U.S. Army was planning to invade. "When the gringo soldiers come they will take my daughter. Please, you take her home with you... She can't be here when they come... Tomela, tomela (Take her, take her)," she begged.

When it finally dawned on me that the mother was asking me to adopt her child, I started waving my hands wildly in front of my face saying, "No, No." Even with Spanish fluency, it was impossible for Suzy to explain to someone who lived in a culture where children are frequently 'gifted' to others, even to strangers, why the Nicaraguan government and the U.S. government would not allow me take a 13-year-old Nicaraguan girl home with me.

I was not sure if she'd even heard of legal adoption, or what would be involved in taking a child out of the country. As far as the distraught mother was concerned, you just give your child to someone if you can't feed or protect her.

In desperation, the mother kept repeating, "tomela... tomela," (take her... take her) while trying to push her toward me. The girl appeared to be shrinking, folding into herself and growing smaller and more terrified by the minute. Holding tight to her mother's hand, she closed her eyes and shook like a leaf, with her wet dress clinging tightly to her shaking body. Suzy began to have trouble translating, as tears ran down her cheeks. With each desperate plea from the mother, her voice quaked as she translated.

Just as desperately, and with true fear, I kept waving my hands in front of my face repeating, "No... no... they won't let me... I can't... no puedo ... no puedo." Chastened, Suzy and I walked speechless toward the center of town, knowing that, after today, we would never see this mother or her daughter again, but knowing also that we would never forget her. The girl would be nearly 50 years old now, if she is still alive. I often wonder what happened to her and to all the women and children swimming with us in the fresh water river. I grew up that day at Potosi. International social work is not all excitement and feeling very capable by helping other people. It is often frustrating... very frustrating... and at times, frightening.

After a Mass, celebrated with all 40 of the remaining residents, we ended our stay by singing what few Spanish songs we knew and marched to the dock. Rob, one of the younger men in our delegation, shinnied up a pole to attach our 8-foot-long banner made from a large white bed sheet, covered with scores of messages of solidarity from the people of Nebraska to the people of Nicaragua. By now I was feeling angry as well as frustrated. The banner had seemed like such a good idea in Nebraska. "The people of Nicaragua will know that there are people in Nebraska who are thinking of them," someone said. What the hell do these people care that there is a bunch of peaceniks in Nebraska thinking of them? I thought. The CIA, our own government, is bombing them! I was about to explode into a silent rant about our naiveté when Suzy called us to get on the bus.

As we approached the bus, Suzy found Carlos, our official soldier/minder. "There were only around 40 people here in Potosi," Suzy told him. "Do you know what happened to the other 200 to 300 residents? They must be around here somewhere. They could not just disappear."

After conferring by phone with Sergio, the Sandinista Army officer in Leon, Carlos and Daniel agreed to take us to a location more inland, near El Viejo, where most of the population of Potosi had been relocated.

"We'll take you to see them," Carlos promised Suzy. "They have started a cooperative farm. You will be impressed with how the Sandinista government is helping them have a better life."

Daniel, the younger soldier, announced with obvious pride, "The families are cooperating to grow crops for the community. They will all share in the profits when the crops are harvested."

When Suzy asked what crops the cooperative was growing, the young soldiers didn't know. They were city kids who grew up in Managua. But they were convinced that the cooperative farm was going to be a big success for the relocated residents of Potosi. They were very serious and sincere about the Sandinista Revolution and how Nicaraguan society was going to change for the better—if everyone did exactly what the Sandinistas asked of them. "Everyone will have everything they need," Carlos assured us.

"On the bus everybody!" Suzy yelled in English to the thirteen of us milling around outside the old bus. "Come on. It's getting late. Say goodbye. Get on the bus.

We're going to find the rest of the people from Potosi. Alvaro, our driver, thinks he knows how to get there." After many hugs and kisses with the people who refused to leave Potosi to relocate inland, we got on the bus and began the slow trip to El Viejo along back roads.

The dirt road, covered with twigs and old leaves, was full of potholes that made the bus bump and sway as we crept along. It was very hot, over 100 degrees. There was no air-conditioning in the bus, so we left all the windows open and cooled ourselves with the large straw woven fans we had thought to buy in the market when we stopped in Chinandega. Fine light-brown dust flew in the open windows, coating our sweaty faces and accentuating all our wrinkles. We looked like escapees from the Asilo de Ancianos (Old-Age Asylum) in Leon.

As we approached a nearly dry river, we realized we had to go down into the river bed to get to the other side. There was no bridge. Since there was hardly any water in the river, Alvaro carefully angled us down the side of the river bank into the river. It was only about four inches deep, so we crossed easily. Suddenly, Alvaro told us all to get out.

"You weigh too much, and I can't get the bus up the opposite bank unless you get out and push," Suzy translated for him, laughing as we struggled to get out of the bus without falling into the water.

While the older women scampered up the river bank, the men and the younger women positioned themselves behind the bus and pushed, getting their sneakers and socks wet and muddy. Alvaro steered the creaking bus at an angle, up the side of the opposite river bank toward the road.

As the women climbed up the river bank, Joyce called out to her friend, Ruth Thone, "Look at you, Ruthie. You look like you've been shot."

"I'm stuck in these pants until we get back to Leon," Ruth replied, laughing at herself and her 'victim of a shooting' look. Ruth's white capris pants had a bright red stain all over her right thigh. She had jumped into the river to join the local women, forgetting that she had her entire prescription of red-coated malaria pills in her pants pocket. She dried off quickly, but the red stain on her pants remained. With no pills left to take, I hope she doesn't get Malaria, I thought. Even simple mistakes like this can be dangerous in the tropics.

Soon after getting back in the bus, we saw cardboard shacks in the distance and quickly came upon the remaining residents of Potosi. "There they are," announced Carlos, the older soldier. "Now, you will get to see how the Sandinistas are helping the people by moving them here to create a cooperative farm."

At first glance, it didn't look like an improvement to me. Unlike the children at Potosi, all the young teenagers running to greet the bus were covered, head to toe, in dirt.

It was the dry season, of course, but there didn't seem to be any water available in the area.

Generally, no matter how poor, Nicaraguans are very clean. Children head off to school in snow-white shirts and navy blue pants or skirts, ironed to a perfect crease. Not here at the new cooperative, however. The children looked like they had been rolling in the dirt. They were covered with sweat, and dirt stuck to every crevice and cut on their bodies. Their hair, matted with fine sand, was not the shiny black hair we saw on children in Leon and Chinandega. Don't they have water? Why are these kids so dirty? Something here just doesn't feel right, I muttered.

One of the young men in our group was a juggler. Rob, a very tall African-American 35-year-old, stood up on what looked like an old railroad baggage cart and began to juggle three and then four baseball-size red and yellow balls. Children appeared from nowhere. They were enthralled, staring up at Rob in amazement.

I watched as Rob struggled to communicate, using gestures, with the pre-teen boys who were begging him to show them how to juggle. Suddenly, I heard a bit of a commotion behind me and turned around in time to see a mother carrying a baby dressed only in a cotton diaper running straight for me.

"Ayudanos," she begged. "Necesitamos medicinas."

After taking a quick look at the baby, I grabbed Suzy by the arm; "Don't go anywhere, I need you to translate."

The baby was struggling to breathe. When I felt her

forehead, it was hot with fever. What hair she had looked like wisps of yellow straw, and the skin that could be seen under the dirt was an anemic white and covered with lesions. At 13-months-old, she was small for her age and very thin, with protruding bones and a swollen belly. Her head was larger than it should have been given the size of her body. Her little body reminded me of a plucked chicken.

Oh God, this is what malnutrition looks like, I thought to myself. If she doesn't have pneumonia now, she soon will. I watched horrified as her chest caved in with every breath.

"This baby is going to die," I whispered quietly to Suzy in English.

"Help us," the mother begged again. "We need medicines."

I wondered what, if anything, we could do for her. Although I was the person in charge of health for our trip, I wasn't a medical volunteer like the doctors and nurses that traveled with us on the flight. I don't have any medicines for babies… plus I'm a social worker, I thought. I don't have the knowledge or skill to diagnose and treat pneumonia… what more can I do? Perhaps I can gather a little money to give her for medicine… but where? We are hours from Chinandega, probably the closest pharmacy.

As I tumbled various solutions over and over in my mind, I heard Suzy translate, "All our babies are dead. Angelina is the only baby under two in the whole community."

Startled, I stepped back and looked around the area; it was teeming with people, but no babies or toddlers. In Leon and in the market at Chinandega, every young woman had a baby in her arms or a toddler on her hip. Boys and girls of 10 or 12 years-of-age walked around with babies balanced on their hips. Babies and toddlers were everywhere you looked in other parts of Nicaragua in 1984, but not here.

It quickly occurred to me that most of the young Sandinista revolutionaries who were now in charge of the country, grew up in cities, and possessed minimal knowledge about what was involved in farming.

What a mess they have made moving over 200 fishermen and their families from the fishing village of Potosi to this patch of dry land! Somehow they expect them to develop a cooperative farm here… with nothing… no water… nothing. This is madness!

Whatever were those running the government thinking? The men here don't know how to feed their families without their fishing boats and nets. Separated from the fresh water river at Potosi where they could wash their clothes and bathe daily, the women here don't know how to keep everyone clean. What a disaster these young revolutionaries have caused. They don't even seem to realize that the babies and toddlers are all dying! I was pissed, while Carlos and Daniel, our two young soldiers, seemed blissfully unaware that the people in front of them were in serious trouble and were not developing a wonderful cooperative farm that would make them all rich.

Proud of their Revolution and speaking in the Sandinista slogans visible on the posters along the main highways, they saw families cooperating to grow crops for the community and sharing in the profits of the harvest. What I saw, looking with older eyes, were malnourished children, dispirited fishermen who didn't know how to farm, and desperate women who couldn't keep their babies alive.

What crops? What harvest? I muttered angrily to myself under my breath, annoyed and frustrated that the baby in front of me would soon die. Angelina doesn't deserve this, I fumed. Don't do stupid things, I wanted to yell at Carlos and Daniel. Don't believe your own slogans! There was no water to be seen, no crops, no fish, only disease… and dust, rising in swirling yellow clouds.

Lost in my own thoughts as the bus bounced along the highway from El Viejo through Chinandega, I realized, at last, that I lacked the knowledge and ability to help these poverty-stricken people. Gazing out the window of the bus, I saw nothing but starvation and death. The land itself looked dead, bone dry with its top-soil blowing in the wind. It was the dry season, of course, the season of want. The rains would not arrive for at least another month to turn the fields lush green again. But in April, too-thin cattle wandered aimlessly around the dry fields, looking more like moving skeletons than animals. Staggering like a drunk to remain upright, one cow looked as if she might, at any moment, take one more step and fall over dead. Farmers had no bales of hay or other feed stacked anywhere that I could see. Apparently, they had no mechanism for feeding their animals during the dry season.

On the thirsty land, there wasn't a blade of grass, only the powdery soil, rising like puffs of smoke when an animal nuzzled the ground looking for green grass to eat. Death prowled the land for animals and humans during the dry season in Nicaragua in 1984, and I had no idea how to stop it.

Still gazing out the window, I sank into despair, fretting over whether we had done any good and questioning why I had come. Why did I think I could help people I couldn't even talk to? Damn it, why is there no feed for the animals in the dry season? I swore silently, as I continued to stare at the dry empty fields with their skeleton-like cows.

Why did Witness for Peace send us to Potosi? Whatever did they think we would learn? The long-term volunteers are very positive toward the Sandinistas. Why would they send us to the cooperative farm near El Viejo where it appears to me that the Sandinistas are harming the people. The families who refused to leave the fishing village of Potosi seem to be in better shape.

As I stared out the window and fretted about the dying cattle, I wondered what the others thought about everything that had happened. I was anxious to talk with the whole group when we got to Managua. I wanted to discuss whether we did the people we met any good…or any harm? Our showing up in their village was, for them, no more than a fun distraction. But, what good did we do?

And what about all those babies and toddlers who died in El Viejo? And what about the mother who wanted to give me her daughter? Imagine us bringing that 13-year-old girl home on the plane with us... like a pet. We need to discuss all our impressions of the trip to Potosi, I thought, sinking further into despair.

After the bus dropped Carlos and Daniel at their Army post in Leon, we gathered our things from the Maryknoll House and headed for Managua. As we bumped along the pothole-filled highway, I heard a song in Spanish playing on our driver's tape recorder called Casas de Carton. I couldn't figure out the exact words, but the song clearly was about the thousands of little 8' by 8' houses made from cardboard shipping containers that we saw dotting the landscape.

When Alvaro stopped the bus to let a herd of 20 cows cross the road, I could see their eyes close-up as they wandered lazily up to the bus, looking at us quizzically through the windows, before being encouraged by their owner to cross over, follow the other cows, and go home.

They reminded me of curious preschool children on a field trip, looking around at the sights, while teachers herd them into what resembles a straight line. Like the cows I'd seen in the fields, these animals were also dangerously thin with rib bones clearly visible under their too large skin. They need rain here, I thought. These animals are starving.

As we waited for the cows to lazily stroll across the Pan American Highway in front of us, I looked off to the side of the road and saw straight through the open doorway of a cardboard house, a casa de carton.

A woman was sweeping the dirt floor, hard as concrete, with a broom made from a tree limb with twigs and a few dry leaves attached. I marveled at how she utilized everything to make her casa de carton livable.

As I watched her, I suddenly realized that all the casas were organized in even rows, making a street between the houses that faced each other. It was a community, not just a bunch of shacks randomly built wherever there was a piece of land. It intrigued me that a woman in such dire circumstances, living in a cardboard house, next to the highway on someone else's land, was so organized. She had next to nothing, but had devised ways to hang the few pots and pans she did have from the cardboard walls inside her little house.

I couldn't live like that, I thought. I wouldn't know where to begin. Later I would learn how fragile these cardboard houses are during the rainy season, when they often collapse on top of families during tropical downpours. But in the dry season they looked livable… at least to my inexperienced eyes.

The farmland we passed was being prepared for planting in advance of the May rains. A team of oxen dragged a man standing on a wooden plow across the field.

A horse, tugging a large tree branch with leaves still attached behind him, was led by a man with a rope. While the oxen plowed the field, the horse leveled it with the tree branch. I was surprised that, in the main agricultural sector of Nicaragua, farming technology had not advanced past two-man plow teams utilizing animal and human power. There were no tractors in the fields, although near a run-down farm building I saw a large red tractor with Russian lettering, rusting and unused, probably for lack of replacement parts, due to the U.S. trade embargo.

I wish Dermot were here, I thought wistfully, looking out the window at the horse dragging the tree branch behind him. Traveling with us he could have explained all these agricultural practices. Dermot had a grant from Title XII of the U.S. Foreign Assistance Act to develop dry beans for the Dominican Republic, so he could have made sense of what I was looking at. I need to ask him about this. It seems so primitive.

I don't see how they can grow enough food to feed everyone in Nicaragua. Managua is a big city and all their food must come from this area of the country, but surely these low-tech practices cannot produce enough.

As I silently contemplated... and was annoyed by... my lack of knowledge about Nicaragua's agriculture, I began to realize how important agriculture is to social work. Maybe we should teach more content about food production in our policy courses. After all, food stamps are administered by the U.S. Department of Agriculture, not Health and Human Services. How could anyone do international social work without knowing a lot about growing plants and animals?

We were coming close to Managua along the Pan American Highway. "There is the Volcano with the big FSLN letters on its side," Jack announced in a loud voice, waking the others and letting us all know we were close to the Mennonite hostel, La Quinta.

The large and sturdy one-story cinder block hostel, La Quinta, was an architectural change from the two-story family homes in Fundesi where we stayed in Leon, from the scattering of foreign-funded tiny 10' x 10' one-story houses made of cinder block with Juan XXIII boldly painted on each latrine along the road to Potosi, and a dramatic change from the thousands of houses made from cardboard shipping containers, which we saw everywhere we looked.

As we settled into La Quinta, it felt strangely like home, with its familiar rocking chairs, colorful cushions, and jute wall hangings. The wooden rocking chairs seemed comfortable after so many days of sitting on metal chairs, leaning against walls, or sitting cross-legged on the floor. The colorful wall hangings brought back memories of women balancing large baskets of fruits and vegetables on their heads in the market in Chinandega. And I now recognized the wall hanging above the door to the kitchen as Momotombo, the perfectly-shaped active volcano that juts partway into Lake Managua, and is visible from both Managua and Leon. I was told that only Japan's Mount Fuji was more perfect in shape.

I could fall in love with this country, I murmured, as I settled back, rocking to the Latin music coming over the radio. As we rocked in our sillas abuelitas and lazily discussed taking cold showers to remove all the sweat, dirt, and dust of the trip, Suzy rushed in to announce, "We have somewhere else to go tonight."

"That woman has more energy than I do!" I muttered. "We have just bounced along the Pan American highway for over three hours, we're covered with sweat and dirt from the open windows of the bus, and now we are supposed to go see something more?"

"I got us into the weekly neighborhood committee meeting that is being held tonight. You will be able to see how they organize the community," Suzy told us.

The thought of sitting through another meeting in Spanish wasn't appealing, but Suzy was so excited about getting permission to see this new technique of community organization, imported from Cuba, that I decided to go.

Joyce, Ruth, and several others came along as well. The rest decided, enough is enough… and headed for their cold showers.

"Stay near me, Ann," Ruth said, as we walked the two blocks along a dirt road to the newly built community center. Knowing she couldn't understand any Spanish, she added, "You'll be able to translate for me."

"Are you kidding?" I replied. "I'm just starting to study the FSI Spanish tapes. I'm only on Lesson Eleven and can't understand most of what they are saying. I can pick out a word here and there, but if Suzy's not translating, you and I are going to have to figure out what's going on from the non-verbal gestures."

When we arrived at the community center, we entered a large square room. It had cinderblock walls up to four feet tall with open space above the walls. The corrugated tin roof was mounted on pillars made of cinderblock that extended up from the walls. The seating arrangement seemed a bit odd. At the front of the room, there were three women and an old man sitting on four folding chairs behind a wooden table facing the rest of the people. In front of the table were nine folding chairs in a single line facing the table, all filled by women with notebooks or stacks of paper in their hands. Around the perimeter sat community members and us. At the back of the room, nine or ten middle-aged men stood with their arms folded glumly across their chests. They didn't seem too happy to be there, but said nothing and just glared.

It soon became obvious that the old man was the titular leader of the neighborhood, but the real leaders were the three women at the table and the nine women sitting in front of them. Each of the women made a report. From the few Spanish words that I recognized, I could make out that one of the women had responsibility for the pre-school (pre escolar). Another oversaw safety, which included a night watch. One headed up salud publica (public health). One by one they made their weekly report of what was happening in their sector of the neighborhood.

"What are they talking about?" whispered Ruth.

"I don't know," I whispered back, "but it may be about an immunization event. I think I heard the word inmunizacion."

Later that night Suzy explained that the Sandinista government had organized all neighborhoods, of about 200 families each, into these local neighborhood committees which reported to regional committees. Regional committees then reported to national committees.

This neighborhood committee system, borrowed from Cuba, was a way for the central government to both know what was going on at the local level and to have a mechanism to quickly communicate with everyone about, for example, an upcoming immunization campaign, or changes in the textbooks to be used in schools. It was also a way, of course, for the central government to keep tabs on anyone who might be organizing against it, and a way to prevent anti-government demonstrations. People who didn't like the neighborhood committees called them the 'Spy on your Neighbors' committees.

This is kind of interesting, I thought, content that I had

decided to come, even though I couldn't translate most of the words. I could, however, see the effects of Liberation Theology, the approach in the Latin American Catholic Church to integrate the weekly gospel and other readings at Mass, into the local community activities. We had observed a Liberation Theology discussion in this same neighborhood before our trip to Leon. Residents then had seemed to be politically aware as they discussed political and social topics using religious language.

Watching with Ruth the neighborhood committee meeting, I realized that the women who, the previous week, had led the prayer groups and the discussions about Mass readings were the same women who were leading the neighborhood committee that evening.

As I watched, I smiled. No wonder the Pope and the Bishops are afraid of Liberation Theology. It is training women in group leadership and community organizing techniques. Looking around I thought, I'll bet those men glaring in the back of the room are the leaders' husbands, uneasy at their wives' new status and power.

As the neighborhood meeting began to break up, there was a commotion just inside the door where we had entered. Two women came in, and members of the community hurriedly gathered around them, since the women were weeping. We motioned to Suzy, who came over and explained that the two women had just, that day, buried their 18-year-old sons, soldiers in the Sandinista Army, who had been killed two days previously by the U.S. backed Contras in a raid on a health center near the town of Condega in the mountains north of Leon.

"Come with us, Suzy. We want to express our sorrow to them," begged Ruth. When Joyce and Ruth, with Suzy's help, began to express their feelings of responsibility to the mothers for the deaths of their two young sons, one mother replied, "Oh no, we understand. We had our Somoza. You have your Reagan." That remark stopped me cold.

The grieving mother was clearly differentiating between

actions of the U.S. government and the people of the U.S. She assumed the people of the U.S. under Reagan lived in a dictatorship like Nicaraguans did under the Somozas from 1933-1979. For those of us who believe that we live in a democracy and are responsible for what our government does, it opened a window into how we, and U.S. foreign policy, are perceived in other countries. We all have a lot more to learn about Nicaragua, but also about our own country.

Our view of the U.S. is so different from how Nicaraguans see us. How will we ever explain to the people back home what we learned on this trip?

The next day, our next-to-last full day in Nicaragua, we met at the U.S. Embassy in Managua with a representative of the American Ambassador. We described to him what we had seen as we travelled to Potosi. He seemed particularly interested and asked lots of questions. When I told him about the yellow striped hair and swollen bellies of the children as we got further north, a sure sign of protein deficiency and malnutrition, he began taking notes.

I explained that the fishermen in Potosi were prevented from using their boats by the CIA gunships in the gulf, so couldn't catch fish for their families, and in addition there was no medical care available for the infants and toddlers who were dying. Suddenly it dawned on me that he could not travel to those areas, and we were giving him first-hand information that he couldn't get any other way.

"I wonder if I should be telling him all this?" I asked myself. He might use my information to hurt those people further. I was conflicted... am I acting as a spy for our Embassy and making it possible for them to do more harm to Enrique and the other children? Or am I helping our Embassy because I am an American citizen and they don't have any other way to find out what is going on in the North. Where do I owe my loyalty, to the U.S. Embassy, to the people we met, or to freedom for all people?

I continued answering his questions, but when we

complained to him about the U.S. treatment of the Nicaraguan people, especially scaring them with explosive noises by breaking the sound barrier, mining the harbor at Corinto, shelling the customs house at Potosi which shut down commerce in the entire northwest sector of Nicaragua, and threatening the local fishermen's ability to set their nets and bring in fish, the representative of the U.S. Ambassador replied, "The Sandinistas are young. They don't know where they are."

Thoroughly dumbfounded by his remark, I asked, "If they are not in their own country, where are they then?"

He immediately replied, "In the U.S. area of influence." That startled us all into silence. You could have heard a pin drop.

What is he talking about? I thought. I have never heard that term before: 'U.S. area of influence.' What the hell is that? Who do these Embassy people think they are acting like they own another country? For the first time in two weeks, I was speechless.

Subsequently, driven by a desire to learn what that term meant, I discovered from Walter LaFever's book, Inevitable Revolutions, that political scientists carve the world up into 'areas of influence.' What we called at that time the 'Soviet Block,' was also referred to as the 'Russian area of influence.' Unknown to most Americans, sectors of the western world (Central America and the Caribbean) are also considered in the 'U.S. Block' or the 'U.S. Area of Influence,' where countries are expected to follow the dictates of the U.S. government rather than the wishes of their own citizens.

All the efforts by the U.S. government to defeat revolutionary forces in El Salvador and Guatemala and to overthrow the Sandinista government in Nicaragua in the 1980s were apparently part of a larger U.S. strategy to strengthen and protect its 'area of influence' in the Cold War fight against the Soviet Block, or the 'Russian area of influence.' Military and economic aid appeared to be based on which party would establish a government friendly to the U.S. and an economy based on western capitalistic free-market principles. I really don't understand my own government, I thought.

We were tired and emotionally drained after two weeks of traveling around the country in our dilapidated green bus. We had listened to interminable lectures, all needing to be translated, about health care, education, and the failed Nicaraguan canal that resulted in the building of the Panama Canal. We had stayed with families in their homes, sleeping on mattresses of straw stuffed into large sacks, and taking cold showers each day. We had tried earnestly to communicate with our hosts to learn about them and their families.

We had worried endlessly, and needlessly, about bugs, not realizing there hadn't been a drop of rain since the previous November and mosquitoes and other flying insects were mostly lying dormant until the rains came in May.

Although we had been afraid of the lack of food and what would be available to eat, we had dined on wonderful dishes of rice, beans, salad, and chicken, using the white cotton tablecloths hanging down in front of us as napkins, since there was no such thing as a paper napkin…or paper anything. We drank all sorts of strange and wonderful fruit juices, and sat together each night enjoying bottles of Victoria beer. But after two weeks, it was time to go home. I'm sure we have all learned a lot, I thought, but I am too tired to think about it. I can absorb and write down only so much information each day. It's going to take me awhile to make sense of this trip… years probably.

As we started packing to leave for Nebraska the next day, Joyce came looking for me. "Ruthie is sick. She can't get up." I went to the women's dormitory in La Quinta to find Ruth curled up in her bed in the fetal position, white and motionless. I discovered from Joyce that Ruth had diarrhea all night and now couldn't move. She looked like she could easily die of dehydration. I had never seen anyone look that white or be that weak, outside of a hospital. Obviously, as the health person on the trip, I had to do something. But what? She couldn't get on the plane tomorrow like that. She didn't even have enough strength to get up and walk. I didn't want to take her to one of the filthy hospitals, and I didn't know any doctors in Managua. Oh God, I hope she doesn't have cholera, I thought, going into a worst-case-scenario panic. Dehydration… UNICEF… public health… I racked my memory and finally remembered that suero (Pedialyte) was what she needed.

I had with me the printed directions from the Center for Disease Control for making suero, the rehydration mixture that UNICEF uses so often to save babies in third-world countries. I grabbed the little piece of paper with the directions from my suitcase and rushed to the kitchen to find someone who could help me make this concoction. It took me awhile to explain to the cook what I needed. Eventually, I got the hand-squeezed orange juice, honey, bicarbonate of soda, and salt that the CDC recipe called for. As I prepared to mix the suero, feeling a bit more comfortable, I decided to try a little small-talk with the cook, since we were alone together in the kitchen.

One of the few phrases I had memorized from my Spanish tapes was Me parece que va llover (it appears to me it's going to rain). With great seriousness (and good pronunciation), I used the line. The cook looked at me quizzically. She clearly understood what I had said, but, after a long pause, eventually answered, "posiblemente." It then dawned on me, looking at her confused face and gazing out the window at the blue cloudless April sky, that we were in the middle of the dry season, and it couldn't possibly rain until the end of May… Oops. I need to concentrate on mixing the suero, and not try to start any more conversations. Will my Spanish ever get any better? I thought, as I focused on my task at hand.

I brought the two separate glasses with me to the dormitory, one containing a mixture of orange juice and honey, the other full of water and salt with bicarbonate of soda mixed in. The directions from the CDC were to drink one sip from each glass alternately, until both glasses were empty.

"Here you are Ruth. This will make you feel better," I told her. "Take one sip of liquid from each glass."

"No, I'm too sick," she whispered.

"Drink it. Sip it." I insisted.

"I can't… " she whined as she lay unmoving, curled up on her side.

"You must… " I insisted again.

Finally, she realized I was not going away and was more of a nuisance than the illness. She pushed herself up to a sitting position and gingerly started to sip the suero. "When I come back, I want to see it all gone," I ordered in perfect mother-speak and left Ruth and the suero in the care of her friend, Joyce.

Several hours later, I felt a tap on my shoulder. When I turned around I found myself face-to-face with Ruth. She smiled and asked, "Can I eat lunch?" The suero had worked its magic and balanced her electrolytes! I was astonished… and relieved.

"No, you can't eat lunch, you are still sick. I'll make you more suero, and later you can eat a little rice," I told her. "You are going to have to drink suero and eat only rice and applesauce until we return to Nebraska."

"You should let your stomach rest. Milk, meat, fat… that will make you sick again." I warned. "You may get hungry by tomorrow night, but at least you won't arrive home looking half-dead."

I'm finally getting into my role as director of health care for the trip, I thought, satisfied that I had, at last, done something right. I should have studied medicine, and not listened to my father's theory that it would be a crime to take a young man's place in medical school and then get married. Why didn't I just sign his contract that I would never marry and study medicine instead of engineering? What could he have done if I later decided to marry? If he were alive today, I wonder what he would think about women's lib… and all the married women working?

The travel agent had had trouble arranging for all 14 of us

to be on the same plane out of Managua, with the large church, medical, and social development groups traveling to and from Nicaragua every day. She scheduled our group on two different flights from Managua into Atlanta. The flight that Suzy and I were on got into Atlanta on time, but the flight that Ruth, Joyce, and five of the others were on was running late. The last flight to Omaha out of Atlanta was about to leave, and only half of our group was on board.

The woman in charge of the flight strode down the jet-way intending to close the plane's door. "We have to wait for the rest of our group," Suzy and I both said, standing in the doorway of the plane, one foot inside the plane and one foot on the jet way. She wasn't about to wait. "No, this flight has to go now. Go sit down," she ordered. We didn't move.

In desperation, Suzy told her, "Dr. Coyne has a patient on the other flight, and she has all her medicines."

I chimed in saying, "My patient is very sick. I have all her medicines here with me, but they put us on different flights. She needs this suero or she could collapse." There was no response, except growing anger on the part of the hapless gate agent. "She's the Governor of Nebraska's wife," I pointed out, hoping this might help.

Overhearing that bit of information, the pilot and copilot, who were sitting with the cockpit door open, stopped checking their instruments and turned their heads to observe the escalating confrontation with the gate agent. The pilot said nothing, but turned his head back to look at the instrument panel, while the co-pilot continued to watch as we stood our ground by telling the furious gate agent we had to wait. After 30 seconds the pilot turned his head back toward me and announced, "That flight has landed. I will wait for the people, but not for the luggage."

I quickly told him, "I don't care about the luggage; I just want my patient with me." The gate agent in charge of the flight scowled and shot Suzy and me an 'I could easily kill you' look and marched back up the jet way to check in our missing group members for the flight to Omaha.

I knew Ruth had given away all her clothes and all her money, so if she got stranded in Atlanta she wouldn't have had even enough money for a phone call, let alone a hotel room (this was before Visa cards).

Plus, we knew there would be a gaggle of reporters and TV cameras in Omaha when we landed. 'Nebraska's First Lady returns from Nicaragua' was the expected headline for the next day. We wanted to make sure the press conference happened.

When the rest of our group came running down the jet way, I grabbed Ruth around the shoulders and hissed in her ear, "Look sick. Look half-dead," and guided her to the seat next to me and gave her the two bottles filled with suero that I was carrying.

At Omaha's Epply Airport, we were greeted by a big contingent of press and ushered into a large room for a press conference. Members of our support group from Nebraskans for Peace were there to greet us. They had been praying and fasting for our safety for the two weeks we'd been in Nicaragua. We, on the other hand, had been eating great food and drinking Victoria beer.

At the press conference, we told the media about all the wonderful people we had met in Nicaragua and the troubles they faced. "We especially miss our good friend, Victoria," someone said. It became our inside joke.

I don't know what good we did, but we learned a lot about Nicaragua and about ourselves… cultures and people are different but not so different. Mothers everywhere care about their children and try to keep them alive and healthy.

The relationship between the government and its people is fraught with errors, power struggles, misinterpretation, other countries' influence, and just plain ignorance. Individuals are affected by the policies of their own government, as well as the policies of other governments. For good or for evil, we all are connected like flies in a global spider's web.

# Chapter 3

# Dr. Roberto Calderon

One night, late in 1984, after returning with her husband from Nicaragua, Carol Stitt called me to ask, "Do you want to go to Nicaragua again with Joel and me?"

Carol and I first met in a classroom, when she appeared, towering over me at nearly six feet tall, looking like a model. She had signed up as an undergraduate student in my social policy class in Fall 1978, but was older, at 24, than the other undergraduate social work students. She had beautiful long dark curly hair, large blue eyes, and a regal bearing. What have we here? I thought, anticipating someone more interested in her looks than in learning. But I was quickly disbursed of that perception when I discovered that she was a good student, exceedingly interested in social policy, and eager to discuss all sorts of ideas in class.

After receiving a bachelor's degree in social work, Carol continued in the graduate program and did her advanced social work practicum under my supervision, while I was on loan from the university to the State, serving as Deputy Director of the Nebraska Department of Public Welfare. By 1984, Carol and I had become good friends despite our 18-year age difference. Plus, we were both married to immigrants who had vastly different life experiences from us and viewed the world from a global perspective.

I was married to Dermot Coyne, then a 55-year-old Professor of Horticulture at the University of Nebraska. He had immigrated from Ireland to study for a Ph.D. at Cornell where we met. Carol was married to Joel Gajardo, a 49-year-old former Professor of International Studies at Cornell. Joel, a tall, thin man with erect military bearing, looked a bit like Don Quixote. He was from Chile and had come to the U.S. after a military junta, supported by the U.S. Central Intelligence Agency, engineered a coup d'état in Chile that killed the elected socialist president, Salvador Allende, in September 1973, and installed a military dictatorship headed by General Augusto Pinochet. Like many of the supporters of Allende, Joel had been rounded up from his home in the middle of the night and kept in the soccer stadium in Santiago, where many of the prisoners were tortured and killed. Joel, an ordained Presbyterian minister with a doctorate in theology, taught in the Catholic Seminary in Santiago. After the coup, the Catholic Cardinal of Santiago intervened when he realized Joel was being held in the stadium, and had him released before he could be killed. Joel came to the U.S. soon afterward.

"Of course I am interested in going back to Nicaragua," I told Carol, and we immediately identified two of our child welfare friends, Heather Craig and Kathy Serghini, as others who might also be willing to go with us to help consult to the government of Nicaragua about the needs of street children. We tried for two years, without success, to get funding for the trip, but finally, in mid-1986, I suggested, "Let's just go on our own."

A Mexican-American nun stationed in Lincoln, Consuelo Tofar, got her religious community to fund her as a translator. The rest of us paid our own way.

The six of us booked our tickets for Thanksgiving break, to leave Wednesday morning and return Sunday night, flying through Miami on Aeronica, the Nicaraguan airline. As we walked toward the gate in Miami to board the plane to Managua, I heard a loud racket right above us and called out to the others walking single file behind me, "Look up there..."

On top of the wall, a few feet above our heads, people of all ages were leaning over the railing yelling and raining trash down on top of us. Cuban-Americans had apparently dressed up their little children in Sunday-best clothes to come to the airport at mid-day on the Wednesday before Thanksgiving, to yell and throw things at people boarding the Nicaragua flight. "Oh my God," I exclaimed as I looked up again and spotted two very angry Cuban men, "Watch out. They are spitting at us!"

Do these rabid anti-communist anti-Sandinista demonstrators somehow think that their offensive behavior will change our minds about going to Nicaragua? Why are they acting like this? ... and in front of their own children!

We raced onto the plane, and wiped the spit off our hair and arms. After the excitement of running a gauntlet to get on the plane, we had an uneventful flight to Managua.

Meeting us at the airport was Dr. Roberto Calderon and two of the resident physicians he supervised. The young doctors had come in their own cars, so they could transport us to their family homes where we would be staying. Dr. Roberto Calderon, our official host, was a U.S. trained radiologist who lived most of his professional life in Houston, but had returned to Nicaragua during the Revolution to help train residents. Dr. Calderon looked like a typical upper-class, 60-year-old Nicaraguan man, who was about 5'5" tall and slightly overweight. He had a dark complexion with dark brown eyes, and his thinning wavy black hair was mixed with grey. We knew he was important from the way the young physicians, in whose homes we were staying, behaved around him. They treated him as if he were a God.

Thanksgiving morning, we were running a little late because there was only one bathroom in the young physician's house. "We have to hurry up. Skip your shower," Carol yelled. "Fernando says we can't be late for our meeting with Dr. Calderon."

"Being on time doesn't matter in Nicaragua," I grumbled, as I rolled out of bed and pulled on my clothes without taking a shower.

"It does to Dr. Calderon," she shot back.

Fernando Lugo, a starkly thin young radiology resident, stood about 5'4" tall with dark curly hair. It was evident that Dr. Calderon had taught Fernando, and all the other residents, that 8:00 a.m. meant 8:00 a.m. and not a minute later. He was not about to be late, as we rushed to get to Dr. Calderon's office on time.

This seems a bit strange in a country where 8:00 a.m. usually means, no earlier than 8:00 a.m., but come within an hour if nothing more important comes up, I grumbled to myself. Timeliness is typically not one of the strengths of Nicaraguan or other Latin cultures. But, if you work with Dr. Calderon, it looks like being on time is required.

At the time, we didn't realize how famous Dr. Calderon was in Nicaragua. I found out later that a hospital in Managua had been named for him, and when my Rotary Club in Omaha wrote a matching grant in 1998 with the Rotary Club in Leon to build 72 houses for the very poor, the Nicaraguan Rotarians named the barrio 'Ciudadela Roberto Calderon.'

When we met that morning with Dr. Calderon to discuss the situation in Nicaragua, he told us how he had come back to Nicaragua from Houston, because of the spreading violence leading up to the success of the Revolution in July, 1979. He described how he and his wife went to sleep each night, not knowing if they would wake up. National Guard helicopters dropped bombs nightly on the city. There were random shootings. But he felt compelled to share his knowledge with newly minted physicians, as they did their residencies in the hospital with him. The depth of his, and his wife's, commitment to Nicaragua was evident.

"Isn't he amazing?" commented Carol as she listened to his tales of providing medical care under battlefield conditions. We all agreed, feeling we were in the presence of someone who truly lived his values.

The following day, a driver in a government van brought Mercedes Flores, the director of children's services for the country, to pick us up. At age 30, she was thinner and taller at 5'6" than most Nicaraguan women, but had the same brown skin, black hair, and mestizo features as other Nicaraguans living on the Pacific side of the country. Mercedes had a bachelor's degree from one of the universities in Managua, most likely from the UCA, the Jesuit 'University of Central America.' She took us to visit a government Centro de Protección (basically an orphanage) for babies and preschoolers in San Marcos, about an hour south of Managua. Located in the hills of Carazo, San Marcos was a pretty little town, one of the three pueblos blancos (white towns, called that because of the whitewash on the houses). Since it was located at a higher elevation than Managua, it was cooler for the babies. At the Centro de Protección in San Marcos, a four-year-old boy called Berto (a nickname for Roberto), served as our guide. He was an odd-looking child with droopy eyelids and one eye lower than the other. Parts of his body on the left didn't seem to match the parts on the right. His back was curved, and when he showed us around, he had to walk on his toes and point to things with his crooked arms.

"Do you think he is intellectually disabled?" I asked Joel.

"He can speak Spanish fine," he assured us. "I can understand him."

Berto was cute and outgoing, tiny with dark skin and eyes, his head topped with very short black hair. I think the orphanage may have shaved the children's heads to prevent lice. Carol and I decided he was mainly physically disabled and probably had normal, or near normal, intelligence. And he certainly overflowed with social skills. During the tour around the cottages and the playground, the four of us English-only speakers just looked wherever Berto pointed and nodded our heads in happy agreement with his descriptions, knowing Joel and Consuelo would fill us in later about what he had said.

Inside the rooms with the babies, there were cotton diapers drying everywhere. The windows at the orphanage in San Marcos were made of heavy slabs of glass about 4" by 30" which slid into metal holders. The educadoras (caretakers) rotated the holders to open the many slabs of glass to let in air. In every window, over every slab of glass, the educadoras had hung diapers and baby clothes to dry. Tiny colored socks were everywhere.

They need a dryer, I thought. How do they ever get things dry in the rainy season? They are having trouble now, and this is November, the end of the rainy season and the beginning of the driest months in Nicaragua. What do they do in June and July when it pours several times a day?

After lunch in a small restaurant in San Marcos, we headed north in the van to visit the Centro de Protección: Rolando Carazo in Managua, which housed pre-teen school-age children. When Mercedes first opened the door of the playroom, the smell of urine washed over us.

As we looked inside, all the children appeared to be screaming at each other, or sitting alone sobbing. The smell and the screaming threatened to overpower us.

"This is sure different from San Marcos," I remarked to Heather, who stood a bit shell-shocked beside me in the doorway. "Dear God, what is going on?" I exclaimed as I stepped through the door and entered the crowded and chaotic playroom. Groups of three or four children, who looked to be between 5-10 years of age, rushed toward each of us, grabbing what body parts they could reach. Looking across the room I could see a young preteen boy, perhaps 12-years-old, pummeling a smaller disabled child, who was screaming for help, but help never came. The two educadoras, who were trying to keep order in the playroom filled with 20 or more children, were too preoccupied with three other children who were fighting on the other side of the room. In a minute or two after we entered, the bigger boy stopped pummeling the disabled child and left him crying on the floor.

Maybe I should go over there and pick him up? I thought. But I realized very quickly that I couldn't move. I was pinned in place by three children who were hanging on both my legs, grabbing for my arms and shoulders and rubbing their bodies against my side, kissing my skin, and moaning unintelligibly. It was bedlam, and I felt like I was being sexually assaulted. "They are so touch deprived," I remarked to Carol. "Look at them," and pointed to the children attaching themselves like leaches, to whatever parts of our bodies they could reach.

Each of us had three or four children grabbing onto our legs and arms while rubbing their bodies against ours. "This reminds me of the film, Snake Pit, about a mental asylum," I said.

To get the children off me, I ordered, "Stand over there. I'll take your picture," pointing to the wall and making picture-taking motions with my camera, in hopes they would understand what I was saying. They dropped their death grips on my legs and moved against the wall, so I could take their picture. I kept saying, "Otra! Otra! (Another! Another!) so they would stay there against the wall and not return to hugging my legs.

In the middle of this bedlam, Mercedes, the head of children's social services for the country, began bragging about the program, while Joel translated. "See how well the children are developing here... This Center of Protection is run by the Sandinista government... You can see how good it is, unlike Centers that are run by the Church... They are so bad... "

I was stunned. All I could think was, who does she think she's kidding? Are we looking at the same children?

I looked over at Carol whose eyes were wide open in shock and disbelief. If the situation wasn't so horrific, I think both of us would have broken into gales of laughter. I didn't dare make eye contact with Heather and Kathy for fear the four of us, all child welfare specialists, would lose it. "These kids are showing signs of being very touch-deprived and are developing abnormally. When they leave here, they will be sitting ducks for sexual predators," I whispered quietly in English to Carol.

As we maneuvered our way out of the playroom, I stopped to talk with one of the two educadoras about a boy who was obviously developmentally delayed. With help from Consuelo, our translator, I mentioned, "I used to work with children like this. Before I taught social work at the university, I worked with intellectually disabled children."

The educadora grabbed my arm begging, "Necesita quedar" (You must stay).

A bit startled, I told her, "No, I can't stay. I have a class Monday. But someday I will come back." My immediate positive response to her request, and my unthinking promise to come back, prompted a crazy idea, which I turned over and over in my mind as I walked toward the van. Maybe I can come back and do a sabbatical here sometime. I don't know when, but maybe sometime… Then it hit me. If I want to live here on my own, I'll have to learn to speak Spanish better than what I do now. I'm still only at Chapter 11 of the Beginning Foreign Service Institute Spanish tapes.

As our driver maneuvered through the Managua traffic to drop Mercedes off at her office, she told us and the van driver that the next day she had arranged for him to take us to visit another children's program in Managua, a Center called La Mascota, that was run by a priest from Spain.

"The government is seriously considering closing it down though," she confided. "It is very bad. In fact, anything run by the Church is usually bad. They don't follow Sandinista ideas and policies."

After the Rolando Carazo fiasco that afternoon, we were prepared for the worst when we approached La Mascota the next day… without Mercedes, who had work to catch up on at her office.

Padre José, a middle-aged priest from Spain, looked more European than Nicaraguan. He was 5'10" tall, slim, with light brown balding hair and hazel eyes. He showed us around the well-cared-for cottages built of cement block, which were painted various subdued pastel colors, unlike the government buildings we had seen, which were universally yellowish beige or unpainted. Basically, the pastel cottages were group homes for about eight children each. As we walked along the sidewalks between the cottages, three boys about 10 years of age waved to us. They kept sweeping the walk outside the pale blue cottage, using as brooms two tree branches still sporting a few leaves. As we got closer they called to us, dropped the branches, and then stood, like young boys all over the world, feet spread apart and flexing their muscles, showing us the big bicep muscles in their arms. One of them pushed and bumped the others gently with his hip to show his muscles were stronger. It was clear they were showing off for us with all their horsing around. They resembled my boys at that age. Relieved to see normal boy behavior, I thought boys are boys, no matter where they are in the world.

Padre José told us that it was lucky we had come when we did. "School is getting over soon, and the boys are cleaning up the cottages, packing, and getting ready to go home. They'll return in early March."

Maybe this is a boarding school rather than an orphanage, I thought as I observed the boys' normal behavior. Maybe they are from rural areas and not orphaned or abandoned like the children in Rolando Carazo. That might explain the difference.

After finishing the tour inside one cottage and watching the boys outside cleaning up their sidewalks in packs of three or four, Carol and I looked at one another suddenly and said in unison, "Boys Town." We broke into giggles.

"It really looks like it," I agreed. Joel asked Padre José if he had ever heard about a place in Nebraska called Boys Town.

He lit up! "Oh yes, we read all about Father Flanagan. We designed La Mascota after Boys Town.

We even have a traveling musical group."

Carol and I burst out laughing. "I thought so," she said.

"Boys Town in Managua," I said. "Who knew? Wait until they hear about this in Omaha."

In the van going back to the agency to pick up Mercedes for lunch, I asked the others, "Do you think Mercedes really believes all the things she told us about how good the government's programs are and how bad La Mascota is? Does she think we can't see how understaffed and awful the program is at Rolando Carazo and how damaged those children appear in comparison to the La Mascota kids? I wonder if she has ever even been to La Mascota herself?"How can Mercedes and I look at the same reality and see it so differently? I thought. Is she blind... or looking for different things?

I'm sure she believes whole heartedly in the Sandinista approach. But can't she see how awful the care is at Rolando Carazo? Are we looking through different lenses, the lens of Sandinista ideology and the lens of social work experience, and focusing on radically different things? This is so puzzling!

During lunch, the four of us social workers, sat wide-eyed in disbelief while Joel translated Mercedes's overview of our trip and the 'truths' about what we had observed those past few days in Nicaragua's children's centers.

How can we see such different realities when looking at the same thing, I wondered? Can culture or ideology affect or even determine what we see? How can our views be so different? Mercedes doesn't look like she is trying to put one over on us. I think what she told us is what she truly sees when she looks at the children in the different centers. "This is making me crazy," I whispered under my breath to Heather, who was sitting equally dumbfounded next to me in the restaurant.

On the ride back late Saturday afternoon to the houses where we were staying, I silently tried to make sense of the distortions of reality... or what I saw as distortions. Is this a classic case of what you see depends on where you stand? Coming from outside this culture, I can easily see what Mercedes is ignoring so she can continue to believe in the Sandinista ideology. Maybe it's cultural or maybe Mercedes doesn't know anything different about child development. Totally unnerved I thought, maybe she's a fanatic... but I don't think so...hmmm.

I began to wonder. What do I ignore when I look at situations through my social work lens? Clearly I focus on certain things because of my culture, training, and experience. I also must ignore other things that don't matter to me or don't seem to fit. How can I tell what I ignore? Are we as child welfare specialists equally distorting reality by ignoring those things not considered important in social work theory and practice? How can I know, since the social work lenses I use to see situations are likely unconscious? How can I see what my lenses are hiding from me?

Fortunately, we got to Fernando's house to shower and get ready for our despedida (going away party), before I made myself completely crazy trying to figure out why Mercedes saw what she saw and believed what she believed.

Sunday morning, we arrived at the Managua Airport in what seemed like the middle of the night, ready to return home to Nebraska. In the distance, we could see a few crop-dusting planes sitting in the dark in the open near the runway, or parked inside hangers made of steel poles and chain link fencing with straw woven through the holes. Three old helicopters sat a short distance away, partially hidden in the shadows, near a brown one-story-tall building with a 30-foot-tall tower built on top of it, which must have been the control tower.

In the middle of the runway, of what looked like a rural Nebraska airport used mainly by crop-dusting planes, stood our plane, a 727, huge by comparison, lit with a spotlight. It looked like a big white bird with Aeronica painted on its sides in red and black letters.

We entered the airport building at 4:00 a.m. and stood in line to show our passports, and to check our bags. The only seats in the waiting room were hard wooden chairs or benches, which were crowded with other passengers, their relatives and friends, and a contingent of soldiers. The outside windows were still dark because of the early hour.

I looked around trying to read the signs on the wall, some printed, some hand lettered. There was the large Sandinista poster with the slogan, No Pasarán! (they will not pass), in red letters showing a soldier in full battle dress, with an AK-47 held across his chest, intent on keeping anyone from passing. Another sign said something about the airport being an ejército, which I knew meant army.

Unfortunately, my Spanish hadn't improved beyond Chapter 11, since my trip in 1984. However, at the bottom of the sign in big letters it said, No Fotos. That was not hard to translate.

As I looked around trying to read the posters, Joel spotted a friend of his whom he hadn't seen for 10 years sitting on a bench across the room. He brought me over to introduce her to me and to find out what she was doing in Nicaragua. I took a quick photo of her and Joel standing against the wall as we chatted. Later, I glanced over and saw a crowd of people gathering in the middle of the room around a familiar short, dark, rotund figure of a man. I wonder where Cardinal Obando y Bravo is going, I thought, as I walked toward them to take a quick photo of him too.

I felt a hand on my shoulder and turned around to face a young man, hardly older than 18, in an army uniform carrying a rifle. "Ven con migo," (come with me) he said, as he and two other soldiers led me at gunpoint toward a back storeroom filled with cardboard boxes piled four to five feet high and smelling of mold. I looked around and realized there were only two small windows overlooking the waiting room, and they were partially hidden by the boxes stacked in front of them. There was only one door, the one where we had entered, and one bare bulb, which hung from a wire and supplied a little light. We were basically in a large storage closet with tiny windows.

"Why did you take a picture in a military installation?" I assumed he asked, because I heard the words foto and militar. The airport at that time was considered part of the military, and the country was still at war with the Contras.

Oh, Christ. They are going to arrest me and put me in jail for this, I thought. I had seen the signs that said in Spanish what I assumed to be "This is a military installation. Do not take photos." But I had ignored them, thinking they were not going to bother a 50-year-old woman who didn't speak Spanish.

How do I know what that sign says? I don't speak Spanish, I told myself, even though I had a very good idea of what it said.

In rapid fire, all three soldiers started asking me questions.

"I don't understand you," I kept pleading, flailing my arms out to the side, palms up. "No comprendo. No comprendo (I don't understand). No hablo español"(I don't speak Spanish).

At that moment, Joel pushed open the storeroom door shouting in Spanish, "Let her go. She doesn't speak Spanish." But they pushed him back into the waiting room and locked the door.

As I watched through the two small windows near the door, the dawn began to light up the sky over the runway with pink and yellow streaks of light. Thoughts of being in a jail cell in Managua when the sun set that evening flashed through my mind. What if they don't let me get on the plane? I thought.

Suddenly my legs started to tingle, and real fear began to creep up my body. What if the others get on the plane without me? I worried that, at 50 years of age, I would be left alone in a jail cell in a foreign country where I didn't understand the language.

I don't think Joel will leave me here alone, I reassured myself, feeling my mouth getting dry. He's been to Nicaragua before. He knows people here. He won't leave me, I repeated, not knowing if that were true or not. I had heard tales of Americans being held in Nicaraguan jails for months on end. What have I gotten myself into?

In my broken Spanish, I tried to answer the lead soldier's questions by saying, "I took the picture because Joel hadn't seen his friend for 10 years. He might never see her again." What I really said was "Nunca, nunca! Diez años. No mas." (Never, never. Ten years. No more).

The soldiers were not impressed. I thought, Oh damn, that didn't work… I may not be able to talk myself out of this mess…

Fear and anxiety began to rise in my chest, and my breathing became very shallow. This is no time for a panic attack… stay calm, stay calm… But my mind raced. I hope they all don't go back to Miami and leave me here in jail… How will I survive alone in a Nicaraguan jail cell… I wonder if the soldiers saw me take the photo of the Cardinal… That might get me in worse trouble…

The taller soldier serving as chief interrogator leaned over the pile of cardboard boxes I was standing behind, came closer to my face, looked me straight in the eye, and demanded, "Otros fotos?"

I hesitated for a second and then whispered in a barely audible voice, "Si, El Cardinal."

There was stone silence as the three soldiers stopped talking and looked at each other. This is it, I thought. They are going to arrest me now. Suddenly I felt the tension in the room drop. Don't move… be still… something is happening, I warned myself and stood perfectly still, leaning against one of the cardboard boxes, clutching it tightly, trying to breathe.

"Váyase (go)," my interrogator said softly and unlocked the door. When the soldiers realized that I had recognized the Cardinal, even though he was not in clerical clothes, they may have decided I knew him or that he knew me. Whatever it was, they didn't want a conflict with the Cardinal.

As I left the interrogation storeroom, I looked around for the Cardinal and made a beeline for him. Before long, I realized that Cardinal Obando y Bravo wasn't going to Miami. He was at the airport, standing beside a young man fleeing the country because of the draft, to make sure the boy was not arrested before he could board our flight to Miami. No one would mess with the Cardinal… not even the soldiers. I stood in line next to him and the young draft-dodger, until they let us onto the plane for Miami. The Cardinal was my new best friend in Nicaragua.

When we landed in Miami, we were greeted by federal immigration and customs agents. Most were Spanish speaking Cuban-Americans who hated Nicaragua with a passion. One inspector seemed to be harassing Joel. Later Joel explained to us that the customs officer was saying nasty sexual innuendo phrases about Carol, calling her names, trying to make him angry, so the customs inspector could arrest Joel for fighting back and not following his directions. We were a bit oblivious, as these were not words we had ever studied in Spanish class. Joel, of course, as a man and as a native speaker, knew well the sexual innuendo that was being spouted by the Cuban-American customs inspector to get an angry response from him. He didn't take the bait. Most Cubans, especially those in Miami who had come to the U.S. as refugees after the 1959 Cuban Revolution led by Fidel Castro and aided by the Soviet Union, were upper class Cubans who had lost all their land and most of their belongings. Some of their family members were probably killed or injured or jailed during the revolution as well. They hated Castro with a passion and hated any country that was aligned with Cuba and the Soviet Union, such as Nicaragua.

As we exited customs, a swarm of 10-15 reporters, several TV cameramen, and two men with sound beams held high over their heads rushed toward us, surrounding us and stopping us in our tracks. "What are they saying in Nicaragua?" one reporter shouted at us. I wondered, why all the sudden interest in Nicaragua at this hour of a Sunday morning.

I yelled back, "There are signs all around saying 'They will not pass,' and there are rumors of a U.S. invasion from the North."

He didn't seem interested. Standing in the Miami Airport on a dark November morning in 1986, surrounded by reporters pushing and shoving to get themselves, their cameras, and their sound booms closer to us, I couldn't imagine what would bring so many national media types to the Miami Airport that early on a Sunday morning to interview us.

"What do the newspapers in Nicaragua say about the U.S. selling arms to the Iranians to pay for the Contras?" yelled another of the reporters. This was the first we had heard of the Iran-Contra scandal.

I just stood there dumbfounded and shrugged.

"We don't have any newspapers with us," Joel yelled back. "I don't know what you are talking about. We left Managua at 6:00 am. The newspapers hadn't come to the airport yet."

The media hoards melted away in seconds.

"What do you think that is all about?" I asked Joel.

"I don't know. Let's go see if we can find a New York Times," he suggested, as the six of us went on the hunt for morning newspapers. "Something big seems to be going on."

# Chapter 4

## Sabbatical

Barging through the door of our house, waving a memo I had received that day at the university, I called to my husband who was sitting comfortably in the other room on the living room couch, "Dermot, they funded it... all of it!"

He looked up silently and stopped writing with his red pen. He'd been busy editing a paper from his new graduate student, Geunhwa Jung. His face clearly said, "What are you talking about?"

"Remember at the beginning of the semester I applied for a UCR grant," I reminded him, but he still looked confused. "University Committee on Research at UNO. They give money to encourage faculty to do research. I wrote a $5,000 grant in January to see if they would fund a sabbatical for me to go to Nicaragua next spring semester to study the child welfare system," I explained, detailing the process, a bit annoyed he didn't seem to remember I had even written the grant.

He put aside Geunhwa's paper and looked up with more interest. "Are you really going to Nicaragua for a whole semester?" he asked, looking a bit hurt that I would leave him for that long, especially since I had just rented an apartment in Omaha in February and was home in Lincoln only four nights a week.

You come and go for weeks at a time with your University projects in the Dominican Republic and Western Nebraska, I thought, beginning to feel guilty for leaving him but also annoyed at his different expectation of me than of himself as a professor.

"I think so," I replied. "They funded a month of language training in Mexico this summer, airfare to Nicaragua, and a computer to take with me in spring 1990," I said, handing him the award memo. "Now I have to figure out how to make this happen."

I had spent 16 months on loan from the university serving as Deputy Director of the Nebraska Department of Public Welfare in 1981-2, but this Mexico-Nicaragua trip represented my first official sabbatical since joining the faculty in 1975. During my time as Deputy Director, I had directed social service and income maintenance programs for the state and helped the department come into compliance with the new federal child welfare legislation, the Adoption Assistance and Child Welfare Act (PL. 96-272, aka Title IV-E), but now it looked like I was going to get the chance to step back from both management and teaching, and instead learn about how child welfare is done in a different country.

"Don't you remember when I went to Nicaragua in 1986 with Carol and Joel to consult with the government officials about the street children?" I asked Dermot, who looked dubious. "I promised then I would come back and help with their disabled children."

Pointing to the award memo in his hand, I said, "Well, it looks like it's going to happen, if I can make the arrangements." He did not look at all happy with the idea of me leaving him for a semester.

Back on campus that spring, I began organizing for the next year's sabbatical in Nicaragua. "What you need is an intensive language course," Dr. Elvira Garcia, Chair of the Foreign Languages Department at UNO, advised me, when I told her about the grant. "Why don't you come to Mexico with us for a month?"

The University of Nebraska at Omaha, where I taught, had an intensive Spanish language program in Cuernavaca, Mexico and sent undergraduate students each summer for a month accompanied by a Spanish-speaking faculty member. In June, I joined Elvira, her husband, and seven undergraduate students for the plane trip to Mexico City and the hour-long van ride to Cuernavaca.

Riding along the traffic-filled highways out of Mexico City, staring at the large volcano looming over the city, I kept encouraging myself, you need to study hard… maybe you can get to advanced intermediate, or at least get good enough to understand something… anything, I fretted. I was doubtful a month in Mexico would make much difference. Languages were not my thing. Getting a workable language would be tough, I knew. Once-a-week Spanish classes at Southeast Community College had not helped much. I needed something more intensive.

On my past two Nicaragua trips, there had been a Spanish interpreter with us, but for the sabbatical, I would be on my own and needed to learn a lot fast. Not knowing the language was what frightened me the most about the sabbatical.

An older undergraduate student, Barbara Ballad, who had left two young children at home with her mother, was my roommate. Barbara was 35, rather old for an undergraduate, but younger than my 53 years. She was tall, perhaps 5'8", and heavy. She looked a lot like the Old Master paintings of peasant women, sturdy and full figured, or the photos of German immigrant women farming in rural Nebraska during the Dust Bowl years of the 1930s. She had brown eyes and dark brown hair, cut short, which framed her round, pleasant face. She looked and acted like a typical middle-aged Nebraska woman, competent and nice. I was delighted to have her as my roommate and not be burdened with a younger student. I was there to study, not to keep a 19-year-old roommate out of trouble. At the same time, I am sure the six younger students were relieved that they didn't have to room with someone older than their mothers! We all stayed, two by two, with different local families in Cuernavaca. Except for our touch-base meetings with Dr. Garcia every morning at the school before classes, Barbara and I didn't have much contact with the younger students. Barbara and I lived with Lupe Espinoza, her mother, Eva Lopez, and Lupe's 16-month-old daughter, Cecilia, in a middle-class house.

Surprisingly, there was a swimming pool in the backyard, which I used nearly every day. Our Mexican 'mother,' Lupe was a very attractive 28-year-old, tall for a Mexican at 5'5," with light skin, a few freckles on her nose, and reddish blond wavy hair which hung in soft curls just above her shoulders. Her blue/brown hazel eyes sparkled when she smiled. She was not what I expected when I envisioned living with a Mexican woman. I think what I had in mind was a 50-year-old, short, overweight woman with straight dark black hair, brown eyes, and brown skin, like a lot of the Mexican women I knew from attending the Spanish Mass in Lincoln. I was to learn later that the racial diversity in Mexico City is like the racial diversity in the U.S. It is only on the Rio Grande border that most of the Mexicans look mestizo.

Cecilia, like all 16-month-olds, was adorable, with short curly brown hair, green/brown eyes, and fair skin. She looked like her mother and had the typical wide gait of a baby who had recently learned to walk. She spent a lot of time in her high chair learning to eat various types of solid food, which she liked to spread on her face and on the tray. She had the confidence of a little one who is well loved. I never heard her mother or grandmother yell at her, although they had to gently redirect her when curiosity got the better of her. Cecilia was a happy little girl.

The day we arrived, after settling our things into our bedroom, Lupe unfolded a map of Cuernavaca, laid it across the kitchen table, and showed Barbara and me where we were in the city and where the school was located a couple of miles away.

She informed us she would take us to school in the morning at 8 am, pick us up at 2 pm to have dinner, and then feed us again at 8 pm. This was different from our American 7-12-6 feeding schedule and would take some getting used to. I knew that by noon each day I would be starving, so the next day I almost signed up for the late morning cultural class in Mexican cooking. But I hate cooking, so I chose art appreciation instead. I'll take Diego Rivera over making tamales any day.

As we looked at the map trying to get our bearings, Lupe called to her mother, whom we had not yet met, "Gordita, ven aqui. (Little fat lady, come here)" Barbara and I looked at one another and froze. Both of us knew enough Spanish to know what gordita meant. We stayed perfectly still, not knowing what to say or do. Soon a plump older woman appeared, smiling and eager to meet us. Lupe introduced us saying, Gordita, te presento a las Anita y Barbara.

Not daring to look at Barbara, all I could think was, I am not calling this woman Gordita, even though she is a little fat. Remembering my beginning Spanish, I said, "Mucho gusto, Señora." I never did hear her called by her first name, Eva. Her daughter always called her Gordita and we always called her Señora. Over time, as we became more acculturated, we realized gordita was a word of endearment, not a slur. But on that first day, it was quite a shock!

Señora Eva Lopez, at 57, was a little older than me and about my height. She had long black hair streaked with grey which she pulled back into a ponytail or rolled into a bun.

She was possibly 20 pounds heavier than me, which made her look shorter. She reminded me of my grandmother, moving quietly about the house, a little bent over with stiff knees, picking up things, straightening pillows, and playing with Cecilia.

At night, she loved sitting in a large soft chair with a pillow, reading the daily newspaper, La Jornada. Once she knew I would be going to Nicaragua in a few months, she told me whenever anything about Managua or other cities in Nicaragua appeared in her paper. Thanks to her, I practiced Spanish by reading something interesting about Nicaragua every evening in La Jornada, rather than being bored reading our text book about how to cook Mexican food. (The chapter on cooking beetles was interesting, although I couldn't imagine ever doing it.) Every day I read about the upcoming February elections in Nicaragua in the Senora's newspaper.

If everything goes according to plan, I will be there in late January, I told myself. Just thinking about going is so exciting. I am such a political animal. Imagine what I will be able to teach my students in social policy when I get back.

The weather in Cuernavaca is always in the 70s, eternal spring they call it, perfect for Lupe's backyard swimming pool. Floating on my back in the cool water every day after school, I often got caught up watching a dozen or more enormous butterflies, flapping their giant wings above the pool.

Many of them were totally black, unlike any butterflies I had ever seen. A few were entirely white. And all of them were huge; I guessed 8" across, if they stopped beating their big rounded wings long enough for me to measure them. Back and forth they would float across the pool, 18 inches above my face, fluttering effortlessly in the air, never bumping into one another, or me. I watched amazed at their size and their grace.

"Everything is so different," I complained to Barbara later that day as we unpacked our suitcases. "Not only is the language different, everything is different. I wonder if it is going to be this strange in Nicaragua?

My mother would kill me if I called her little fat lady."

A few days after we arrived, we heard loud shouting in Spanish coming from one of the upstairs bedrooms. Barbara and I bounded up the stairs to find Lupe and her mother cowering in the corner of our bedroom, flailing their arms wildly at one white and two black giant butterflies that were flapping back and forth lazily across the room. "They won't hurt you," I yelled in English above the din. "I've been swimming with them flying overhead." My attempt at reassurance didn't seem to help, since neither of the women could understand anything in English when they were that upset. They continued to flail at the flapping wings with their arms over their heads, like referees calling time-out in a football game, and yelling something unintelligible at the butterflies.

Why can't I learn this language better, I fumed silently. In Nebraska, I could cope with someone terrified of a butterfly. Why does it have to be so difficult here? I feel like a 5-year-old who can't do anything.

When Barbara reappeared in the door of our room minutes later wielding a broom, Lupe and her mother stopped shouting and clung to each other in the far corner of the bedroom, as we took charge of ridding the house of butterflies.

"Don't hurt them," I pleaded with Barbara. "They are not dangerous. They are beautiful. They are not going to bother anything." Barbara started sweeping gently in the air with the broom, trying to move the air to push them toward the door, hoping they would fly out the open window at the end of the hall, where they had apparently entered. The white one complied, but the black butterflies would have none of it. One parked himself high in the corner of the bedroom, against the ceiling, opposite from where the two Mexican women… our defenders… were still cowering. The other huge black butterfly continued to lazily float from corner to corner of the room, swooping up and down, while avoiding the broom Barbara was whooshing gently in all directions.

"We are going to need a step ladder," I called out to Lupe, still cowering but not as frightened. I made climbing motions in the air with my hands like climbing a ladder, so she or her mother might understand what I wanted. Lupe led her mother out the bedroom door, and they fled downstairs to the kitchen to find a ladder. In two minutes, Lupe produced a large ladder. The butterfly I was targeting hadn't moved from its perch in the uppermost corner of the bedroom.

I climbed up to the very high ceiling and told Barbara, "Ok, I'm going to see if I can get him to fly down, and you whoosh him and the other one out the door," hoping we didn't hurt them in the process. It worked after a few tries, and the last we saw of the black butterflies was them heading for the safety of the swimming pool. We shut the hall window and dissolved into laughter.

"They are supposed to be taking care of us," sputtered Barbara between laughs, referring to our Mexican mothers.

"And people complain about Americans being afraid of bugs," I replied. "Butterflies, harmless giant butterflies… it's not like they were poisonous spiders."

The next 'acculturation event' wasn't so funny. One afternoon the following week, as I sat studying at the kitchen table and watching Lupe feed supper to Cecilia in her highchair, Barbara came through the back door crying and looking disheveled. "What happened?" I asked alarmed, as she sat on a chair beside me, across the table from Lupe and the baby. I quickly looked her over from head to toe for signs of cuts, broken bones, or bruises. She clearly had been roughed up, but didn't appear to be seriously injured.

"I went for a walk… where we all walked last Sunday," she sobbed, looking at me. "A police car stopped… that short creepy policeman that was eyeing us yesterday told me to get in… he drove around the city for 20 minutes or so… he tried to tell me I should come with him… "

"I couldn't understand anything… he spoke so fast… then he headed out away from the city… I didn't recognize any place… I was sure he was going kidnap me or rape me."

Lupe couldn't understand much of the English, but it was evident from the look on her face that she could understand from the fear and the crying and the tattered and dirty clothes what had happened.

Barbara continued, "After a while, when he turned a corner I suddenly saw someplace I recognized." She lifted her head and faced me. "It was the road where we walked last Sunday afternoon with the other students, over near the bridge," she said.

"What did you do?" I asked, wondering how she had escaped the car and made it home from there in one piece.

"When he slowed down, I opened the car door and jumped out... I fell, but I rolled onto the grass... then got up and ran toward the road and the bridge that I recognized."

"Did he chase you," I gasped, realizing he had control of a small white Volkswagen Bug with Policia painted on its side, and she was on foot.

"I don't think so. I just ran. I didn't see him after I jumped out of the car. Thank God I knew where I was," she said, regaining her composure and strength.

Lupe intervened. "Don't ever get into a car with a policeman," she said in mixed English and Spanish. "They are not safe. Most have only three years of education. Policemen are dangerous."

She then began instructing us, making sure we understood her words about who was safe, who wasn't, and what to do. "If you get chased, run into any store and shout," she recommended. "He won't follow you in there and the shopkeeper will protect you. Don't try to run home. Go into a store... "

"Are all the policemen dangerous?" I asked, stumbling over newly learned Spanish words.

"Most policemen have gone to school for only three years," Lupe explained... "They don't make much money... they will rob you. Also, never get into a taxi that has two men in it, especially two in the front seat. Those are ladrones (robbers)," she instructed. "And never ever get into a police car, even if the policeman orders you to get in. Run-away towards a store and yell."

After this, I will find it hard to believe the policeman is my friend, I thought.

Lupe sat quietly at the table across from us, and began again to spoon something soft and orange into Cecilia's mouth. We sat speechless, trying to wrap our minds around the idea of policemen as dangerous robbers and rapists. Finally, Lupe put down the spoon and said with an even more serious voice, "Stay away from the soldiers. They will kill you." That focused our attention!

Lupe wanted to make crystal clear that we completely understood what she was saying. She explained with the English words she knew and the Spanish words she thought we knew.

"If you see a soldier, do not talk to him. Go to the other side of the street. He could hurt you. Many Mexicans have been killed by soldiers. People just disappear and are never found. They are called desaparecidos." That put the fear of God in both Barbara and me.

We headed upstairs to treat the scrapes on Barbara's arm and both knees, which were beginning to ooze and hurt. For someone who had jumped out of a moving car, she looked good; other than the scrapes on her knees and right arm from her roll on the pavement, she had only a single blue-tinged bump on her forehead. We both had Band-Aids and antibiotic ointment with us in first-aid kits, so before long she was patched up and ready for bed.

"I wonder if Dr. Garcia knows all this?" I asked Barbara as we lay in our twin beds talking over the day's activities. "You had better tell her about the policeman and what happened," I said, rolling onto my side and propping myself on my left elbow so I could see Barbara, wondering what Elvira Garcia would do. "I think you need to tell her, so she can instruct the other students to stay away from policemen, two men in a taxi, and soldiers." I lay down again and after a few minutes asked, "Do you think Dr. Garcia knew how dangerous policemen were and didn't tell us? Or do you think she just didn't know?" Barbara didn't answer. She had fallen asleep.

It occurred to me at that moment that taking students to a foreign country was a lot of responsibility for a professor. That was reinforced the following morning at our daily touch-base gathering at the school when two of the young female students proceeded to excitedly tell us all about going to Mexico City on a lark the night before in a car with some young Mexican males they had met that day. As I listened to the two students unsuccessfully try to convince a very angry and sputtering Dr. Garcia that there was nothing to worry about, I was grateful I was not in Elvira's shoes as the professor in charge of us all.

We all managed, somehow, to survive the month of language study abroad and returned intact to Omaha with improved, if not perfect, language skills. It made me aware that not only is the language different in a foreign country… everything is different. To survive, I would need to understand how and why people acted the way they did.

Will Nicaragua be the same as Mexico? I wondered. Will I have to be careful around the police and the soldiers there too? I remembered our two soldiers in 1984 accompanying us to Potosi. Carlos and Daniel didn't appear dangerous, despite their AK-47s, I thought. Maybe this is a Mexican thing.

Back at UNO during fall semester, I began planning the precise details of my sabbatical in Nicaragua.

Because the U.S. government had sent funds to the Contras that were trying in the 1980s to overthrow the Nicaraguan government (until the Iran-Contra debacle in 1986 put a stop to the U.S. funding), Nicaragua did not have an Embassy or Consulate anywhere in the U.S. to issue visas.

I want to stay in Nicaragua from mid-January to mid-July, but how am I going to get a visa to enter Nicaragua in the first place? I thought. The visa is going to have to be issued in Nicaragua and sent to me, I realized, as I worked over all the alternatives in my mind.

A friend of Elvira Garcia's suggested I call an American non-governmental organization, Friends of Nicaragua. She had heard the NGO was in Managua, and she thought they might be willing to get me a visa. I had never heard of the organization before, but I had no other connections to help me. The Nicaraguan government workers we had met in 1986 were no longer in their government jobs, and Joel didn't know how to reach them at their homes. His friend, and former Nicaraguan Foreign Minister, Fr. Miguel D'Escoto, had left Nicaragua for a mission in a different country. I was stuck.

It looked like this unknown NGO was my only way to get a visa, as the closest Nicaraguan Embassies were in Canada or Mexico. I went ahead and called Managua and talked to Sharon Lawlor, a young American woman working for the organization in Nicaragua. "I can't come on a visitor's visa, since I will stay longer than the 90 days," I explained to Sharon, who was spending a year in Nicaragua working with single mothers in a poor barrio in Managua. "I need your help getting a work visa. Also can you find me someplace to stay and a child welfare agency where I can volunteer?" There was no Internet in 1989, so all communication with Sharon in Managua was done by phone. A letter would take weeks, if it arrived at all.

There were very few fax machines in Managua, but Friends of Nicaragua did have one, according to Sharon. However, it printed on shiny paper rolled around a metal spool like toilet paper, and was hard to use. When Sharon sent a fax message, she told me, the fax machines frequently didn't 'shake hands' and connect. When she received a fax, the shiny paper often got too hot and turned black while it was printing. Phone calls were much easier.

Every week during fall semester, I called Sharon by phone. "What are you doing about my work visa?" I'd ask her repeatedly, trying to figure out the date when I should get a plane ticket and leave for Managua.

"They're working on it," she always answered. But, no visa ever came.

Fall Semester flew past, and suddenly it was Christmas, and then mid-January. "What are they doing down there?" I complained to Dermot after we returned from a week of visiting his project in the Dominican Republic. He had taken me with him to see the bean experiments and the new research building his USAID project had built. By then, I was officially on sabbatical but not going to Nicaragua in January—or any time soon if the visa didn't come.

I called Sharon in Managua again toward the end of January.

"What is wrong?" I demanded. "Why don't I have a visa?"

"They are not issuing work visas now," she informed me. "They are too busy with visitors' visas for the reporters and other people, like President Carter and members of the UN, who are coming to observe the election."

"When did you apply for the visa?" I asked, wondering if Sharon had ever even done it, or was just stringing me along.

"Oh, I applied for it last September," she told me. "The secretary at Immigration told me then it would be ready in about two weeks."

"Did you believe her?" I asked.

"No. They promise things to get rid of you," Sharon explained.

"What am I supposed to do?" I fretted. "I don't want to give back the $5,000 grant. I've already paid to go to Mexico for language school and bought the computer."

"Maybe you should try to get a visitor's visa from the Nicaraguan Embassy in Mexico City," she suggested. "We can get it extended for you here in Managua when the 90 days are up. Come in on a visitor's visa."

Now she tells me, I muttered, as I angrily put the phone down. I should have thought of that… What is wrong with you? I muttered. You can't just sit around waiting for others to make your arrangements. Figure something out! I was pissed, more with myself than with Sharon.

The Nicaraguan election for president was to be held in mid-February 1990. The economy of Nicaragua was in ruins, with 35,000 percent inflation, caused by all the fighting between the Contras and the Sandinista Army.

Many of Nicaragua's wealthy and middle class young men (and some of their parents) were living outside the country, the youth to avoid the draft, the parents to avoid the Sandinista's policies that affected their businesses and professions. Much of Nicaragua's wealth was being sheltered in U.S. dollars, safely invested outside the country. Over 55,000 Nicaraguans had been killed during the 1980s, especially in the rural areas, and the people everywhere were sick of all the violence.

The U.S. pledged over $1 million, through the National Endowment for Democracy, to provide professional marketing and management help for the presidential campaign of Doña Violeta Barrios de Chamorro, the widow of Pedro Joaquin Chamorro, a national hero. When Señor Chamorro was its editor, the national newspaper, La Prensa, turned against the government, so President Anastasio Somoza, Jr. had him murdered. In fact, the death of Señor Chamorro, and the disappearance of money donated to Nicaragua after the 1972 earthquake, are thought by historians to be the precipitating factors that led the Catholic Church and the business community in Nicaragua to withdraw their support for President Somoza and support his overthrow by the Sandinistas, which occurred in July 1979.

In 1990, Doña Violeta headed the ticket of a newly formed party, the United National Opposition (UNO), which was made up of 14 political parties, ranging from four parties on the far right to the communist party on the far left. They came together for the sole purpose of defeating the ruling Sandinista Party which had been in power for the 11 years since the Revolution had ousted the dictator, President Anastacio Somoza, Jr.

Sra. Violeta Barrios de Chamorro was a handsome woman of 60, a grandmother with silvery white wavy hair and upper-class bearing. She was tall and regal, taller and slimmer than most Nicaraguan women, and during the campaign was always dressed in an elegant white silk suit, no matter the temperature. Doña Violeta used the color white as an important marketing technique in her presidential campaign. With white, the symbol of the Virgin Mother, her campaign used color as an unconscious association of Doña Violeta with the Virgin to energize voters to embrace her as a mother who could bring peace to the country.

She could bring the fighting factions back together into a peaceful family again. In her own family, she had a son and daughter who were Sandinistas and a son and daughter who were anti-Sandinista, but she insisted they and their families come to her home for dinner every Sunday and talk to each other about something other than politics. She could do the same for the country. She could bring peace and an end to the draft. Nicaragua could again function as a family.

Doña Violeta de Chamorro suffered from rheumatoid arthritis, and shortly before the campaign had broken her kneecap in a fall. She couldn't walk well, but using crutches she could stand and speak with authority. She conducted her campaign standing in the bed of a small white pickup truck, called a camioneta, holding onto metal bars installed behind the cab. Standing dressed all in white, in the bed of the white camioneta, she looked a bit like the Pope, also dressed in white, standing and waving through the open top of his white Popemobile. Doña Violeta Barrios de Chamorro, a firm believer in democracy and moderation, was a powerful candidate for her cobbled together political party, especially when getting rid of the draft and ending the U.S. embargo became the focus of the election.

In early 1990, reporters flooded Nicaraguan Embassies and Consulates all over the world seeking visas, so they could report on the election or serve as poll watchers. Since election shenanigans were expected, the Carter Center was sending many poll watchers. President Carter himself would come with them. The UN, for the first time in its history, was sending a delegation to observe a member state's election.

I'm not going to be able to get down there before the election, I realized. But I don't want to sit around here for six weeks doing nothing until the end of February. "I'm going to study Spanish again at the language school in Cuernavaca all during February, wait until the election hubbub is over, and then get a visitor's visa," I told Dermot as I prepared to go to Mexico again. "It won't hurt to study Spanish more before I have to use it. Plus, I'm sure someone at the language school will know how to find the Nicaraguan Consulate in Mexico City. On weekends, I'll have time to go to Texcoco to visit Yolanda at CIMMYT where Pancho works," I said, really looking forward to seeing her again. Yolanda and I were very good friends despite our difference in age. She and I had worked together organizing and developing the Hispanic Center in Lincoln the entire four years Pancho was studying for his PhD.

Pancho, like Dermot, was a plant geneticist, but he developed corn varieties, while Dermot developed disease resistant dry bean varieties. Yolanda and I were both mothers, although my six children were a generation older than her five. We both loved to be involved in politics and social change. In fact, in Uruguay, she and Pancho had gotten into difficulty with the government by carrying out social action activities when they were students together in Montevideo.

In late January, after a bumpy plane ride from Houston to Mexico City on Continental, I caught a bus to Cuernavaca to study Spanish for another month. Fortunately, Lupe had an empty room in her house for me, even though she also had another student, Hector Gonzalez, a Mexican student who was doing an internship at a local power plant as part of his engineering degree from a Mexican university.

As expected, the weather was still 'eternal spring' even in late January, and the butterflies were still busy circling the swimming pool. Since I left in June, Cecilia's hair had grown longer and she had learned to say 'agua' and 'no' and was walking very well and getting into everything. She could climb up and down the stairs with her grandmother's assistance. Settling back into Barbara's and my old room, I felt like I had come home.

The language school had much smaller classes than in the summer, and rather than university students, older professionals were there struggling to learn Spanish. One of my two classmates,

Franz Neuhart, worked for a German airline as a steward. They sent him to language school in Cuernavaca, so he could better assist Spanish speakers on various flights. Franz's and my Spanish was equally weak, so we ended up in the same low intermediate class. However, like most Germans, he knew how to speak English well.

Franz had been working for the airlines for 5 years. He primarily worked domestic routes, but wanted to be able to get onto the longer and better paid international routes. He would need Spanish if he hoped to get assigned to the Berlin to Madrid flight, not to mention the flights to Buenos Aires or Santiago. While English served well for most Europeans who didn't speak German, travelers from Spain or Latin America were often not fluent in either German or English. He needed Spanish.

At age 28 and 6'1", Franz looked every inch a German. He had light blond hair which hung down his forehead almost to his deep-set bright blue eyes. From his broad shoulders, strong athletic arms, and slim physique, it was evident that he worked out every day. I wouldn't have been surprised to learn that he had played on a European football team, perhaps as a goal keeper whose hands could reach above the crossbar when he leaped like a gymnast to prevent a goal. He was very handsome and all the young women at the language school, students and teachers alike, buzzed around him like bees.

The Berlin Wall that separated West from East Germany had come down just three months before on November 9, 1989. Border controls were less strict, so Germans from East Germany were moving to the West, which bothered Franz to no end.

"They don't know how to work, you know," Franz told me. "They never had to study or prepare for a job.

Jobs were just given to them by the communist government. They will ruin West Germany, because they'll all go on welfare. West Germany has really good social welfare programs, and they will bankrupt all of them," he said, clearly indicating that these programs didn't belong to the 'new' Germans coming over from East Germany. "We paid for all those benefits," he said with emphasis.

I thought to myself, Dear God, this sounds just like what the Irish said about the Italians in Boston in the 1950s and what white Americans say about Mexicans now. Why are newcomers always seen by the present inhabitants as worthless, lazy, immoral, and out to get what belongs to the inhabitants who got there first? Why do we humans think like that?

It surprised me that Germans said the same thing about fellow Germans. They look alike, for God's sake. They are not a different color or speak a different language. They all are German. I was stunned. When I saw the wall come down on TV, I thought all the West Germans would be happy to be reunited with Germans from the East. Apparently not. I often wonder what Franz thinks today about having had as his President, Angela Merkel, who grew up in East Germany.

Everyone at language school in Cuernavaca, whether Mexican, North American or European, was focused on the Nicaraguan election. As the day approached, all the polls coming out of Nicaragua predicted that the Sandinistas would win, and win big.

La Jornada and other newspapers in Mexico wrote editorials about what an expected Sandinista victory would mean going forward. American polling organizations, such as Gallup, had hired hundreds of young Nicaraguan women (not realizing most Nicaraguan women tended to be Sandinistas) as poll takers, and the poll numbers looked extremely good for the Sandinistas, perhaps as high as 2:1.

The night before the election, Mexican TV ran a long news program from Managua, showing workers preparing the polling stations and young people beginning to line up to vote, trailed by TV cameras, photographers, and multiple reporters with microphones or small pocket notebooks, anxious to interview everyone and anyone who looked like a Nicaraguan voter. What surprised me was the age of the voters. Most looked like high school students. Nicaraguans can vote at age 16, and there were lots of 16, 17, and 18-year-olds enjoying all the attention coming from the international press.

Lupe, Señora Lopez, Hector, and I watched, on TV, the masses of people getting the country ready to vote the next day. It looked like the entire country of Nicaragua was out on the street, despite the late hour. Young women with babies in their arms, grandmothers holding onto toddlers, and fathers with young children on their shoulders were all milling around the international media, enjoying the fun and excitement of an election block party. Looking at the jumble of people, I could clearly see Nicaragua's median age of 15: half the residents under and half older than 15. These voters looked very different from the more elderly voters in the U.S. where the median age at that time was 31.

Nicaragua was chock full of children and youth, and they all seemed to be out on the street that night, celebrating as if the election had already been won. The teenagers, experiencing their first opportunity to vote in a national election, were everywhere singing and dancing in the streets of Managua. Even in the smaller cities, when the TV would shift to Leon or Granada or Esteli, teenagers were everywhere putting on a show for the TV cameras.

"It looks like a national Block Party," I said to Lupe. "Wouldn't you just love to be there?" It reminded me of downtown Lincoln on a football Saturday, when 90,000 fans are partying in the street on their way to a night Nebraska Cornhuskers football game.

In addition to the international press, the country was full of election monitors from all over the world, including President Jimmy Carter himself, a large contingent of poll watchers from the Carter Center, and the delegation from the United Nations. The poll watchers were not as visible as the teenagers on Mexican

TV, since most were monitoring rural voting stations around the country, looking for irregularities… not dancing in the streets.

"That's where my visa went," I jokingly told Hector, pointing to an American ABC-TV reporter interviewing a young woman, who, like many others, said she intended to vote for the Sandinistas.

On the day of the election the turnout looked enormous. Huge crowds were shown by Mexican TV lining up to vote all day. The lines remained long as people waited two or more hours to be able to vote and then dip their little finger into the purple ink.

We watched until 10 pm and then went to bed, confident that La Jornada would carry the news of a Sandinista victory the next morning, along with interesting comments for me to read and translate.

Instead the headlines in big bold black letters read: GANO DONA VIOLETTA (Doña Violeta won). We were stunned! Everyone at language school that day walked around like zombies, muttering to themselves. No one could concentrate on their studies. "What do you think will happen?" one of the teachers asked me, knowing I was preparing to do a sabbatical in Nicaragua.

"I don't know. And I have no idea what I am going to do," I replied. "With a change of government, all the personnel in the Embassies and Consulates will change. Now, I may never get a visa!"

That reality began to set in. What if I can't get a visa, will I have to give the $5,000 back to the university? I have already spent it on language school and the $3500 computer. Maybe I should go home. But I don't want to leave. Nicaragua will be very interesting after such a dramatic shift, including how they handle the child welfare system. Now is the time to be there. I need to get a visa.

# Chapter 5

# Getting a Visa

What am I going to do? Out of money for another month at language school, but not wanting to go home, I was determined to stay in Mexico until I could get a visa. This is my last chance to spend my sabbatical in Nicaragua. Maybe Yolanda will take me in while I try to get a visitor's visa in Mexico City. I called her from Cuernavaca the night after the stunning Nicaraguan election.

"Sure, come stay with us," Yolanda said happily when I called. "I go into Mexico City a couple of times a week to the British Embassy for English classes. You can ride with me and go from there by taxi to the Nicaraguan Embassy to get your visa."

I was so relieved. There was still hope I would get to Managua and not have to return home, without ever getting there.

When my Spanish classes in Cuernavaca finished the end of February, I moved to Texcoco to live with Yolanda, her husband Pancho, and their five kids. Both Yolanda and Pancho, like many residents of Uruguay, were of Italian descent and communicated with the energy and emotionality often seen in Italians from northern Italy, where their grandparents grew up before immigrating to Uruguay.

With her light skin and blond hair, Yolanda often passed as an American in Lincoln, until she opened her mouth to talk or got mad at another driver and began shooting out Spanish words with the rapid fire of a machine gun. She and Pancho had been student radicals together as undergraduates in Montevideo, and Yolanda retained her enthusiasm for social change. She was particularly intrigued with the Nicaraguan Revolution in 1979, believing, rather uncritically, that the Sandinistas were almost saintly. Their loss in the national election came as a huge shock to Yolanda, who was depressed as well as angry about the results. I was also surprised by the election, but mainly angry that I had yet another barrier preventing me from getting a Nicaraguan visa.

Along with many of the children living on the CIMMYT campus in Texcoco, the four older Crossa children took a CIMMYT van to a dual-language school in Mexico City, 30 minutes away. All Yolanda's children, except the baby Mateo, spoke English like natives, having lived in Lincoln so long. One son was even born there.

Texcoco's Centro Internacional Mejormiento de Maiz Y Trigo (International Center for the Improvement of Corn and Wheat) was a self-contained campus, with its own water supply, and included research labs, greenhouses, and cottages for researchers and their families, built around a large playground fitted with slides and swings. There were acres and acres of land for experimental plots of corn and wheat, where the famous plant breeder and 1970 Nobel Peace Prize winner, Dr. Norman Borlaug, worked.

Dr. Borlaug, by developing disease resistant wheat varieties, was known as the father of the Green Revolution. The varieties of disease resistant wheat that he and his team developed doubled wheat production and staved off starvation in many places, notably Pakistan and India. In total, Dr. Borlaug may have saved about a billion people from starvation.

The research scientists working at CIMMYT were from all over the world. Most were young PhDs with small children. Every family had at least one maid, and some had nannies as well.

Shortly before I arrived, the wife of one of the Chinese scientists had given birth to twins, which was causing them worries about ever being able to go home to China. The couple already had an older child and were not allowed by their government to have a second child, let alone a third.

Oftentimes, after her four older children left for school on the van with other kids from CIMMYT, Yolanda and I would spend many mornings scrubbing vegetables and fruits with soap and the purified water piped into all the buildings on the CIMMYT campus. Most water in Mexico, at least at that time, was full of bacteria. A common saying was, 'In Mexico there is not a drop of water fit to drink.' Fruits and vegetables irrigated or washed in contaminated water had a residue of bacteria on their skin or rinds that Yolanda was determined to scrub off before she cut the oranges or peeled the carrots and prepared them for dinner.

Mateo, born in Mexico, was two years old and babbled constantly. He liked to play with his toys and talk with me and Esperanza, the maid who came every afternoon so Yolanda could go to English classes or go shopping. I decided Mateo would be my Spanish teacher, until Yolanda overheard me mimicking him.

"Don't copy him. He's speaking Chinese!" she called out from the other room.

On another occasion when he kept annoying his mother, I scolded him in perfect Spanish, "Mateo, leave your mother alone. She is taking a nap." I don't know if he or I were the most surprised. Where did that come from? I asked myself and decided that mother words in all languages are imbedded in mothers' brains. I hadn't studied those words or those phrases; they just appeared when needed. I must be picking up this language, I thought with some pride… and relief.

On the Monday after I arrived at Yolanda's, we drove from Texcoco into Mexico City, where I came face to face with what is certainly the worst traffic in the Americas, worse than Boston or even New York. The roads were six lanes across, packed bumper to bumper, and the drivers seemed dedicated to preventing one another from merging. But, if given the slightest bit of space, they'd cut one another off with impunity. Fender benders were a common sight. Most of the traffic moved much too fast, except for the occasional truck which could barely move at all, creeping along, creating a hazard and clouds of pollution.

I couldn't imagine what the traffic and pollution would have been like if Mexico City had not enacted a special traffic control policy—cars with license plates ending in an odd number could be driven into the city only on odd dates. The same with even numbered license plates. They could go only on even dates.

When we arrived at the British Embassy where Yolanda was taking advanced English classes, she pointed to a tree on the corner of the parking lot and said, "Go over there by that tree and hail a taxi. Tell the cab driver the Nicaraguan Consulate is near the Satélite and show him the address."

"Near the what?" I gasped.

"Satélite," she answered, taken aback by my confusion. "Don't you know Satélite?" She wrote the word on another scrap of paper and handed it to me. I clutched it tightly, and said out loud, "Satellite."

"No, no. Satélite. Repeat after me, 'sa TELL i tay.'"

When she finally was convinced I could say it well enough to be understood, she sent me to the street corner to hail a cab and find my way to the Nicaraguan Consulate, then turned and raced into the imposing British Embassy, late to her class in Advanced English skills. She would be there for two hours.

Off I went alone in a cab, across one of the biggest and most dangerous cities in the world, with the language skills of a 3-year-old, clutching a piece of paper with the address of where I was going and the address of the British Embassy so I could get back. Today I wouldn't dream of doing this by myself in Mexico City. But I was desperate.

Oh my God, look at this traffic. What if we have an accident? What if we get stranded? How will I find Yolanda?

After only two attempts at Satélite, the driver finally understood me and found the Nicaraguan Embassy, which was in an elegant, 100-year-old home on a tree-shaded side street. The neighborhood looked strangely familiar, since the houses reminded me of the Brownstone mansions on Commonwealth Avenue in Boston, built in the late 1800s.

After climbing concrete steps toward the large wooden front door, I spotted a hand lettered sign next to the doorbell: Cerrada. The Embassy was closed. Now what? I thought, as I walked down the steps and away from the closed Nicaraguan Embassy in search of another cab. I kept a firm hold on the piece of paper with the address of the British Embassy, and walked three blocks toward an 8-lane-wide major highway teeming with speeding cars.

Trucks lumbered by more slowly than the cars and belched black smoke whenever the driver shifted gears. No wonder Mexico City has such bad air. It makes my eyes sting all the time. I wish Mexico City was more like Cuernavaca, with its breathable air. Mexico doesn't control emissions from its trucks. Look at this… visible air… you can actually see it! I also could taste it, and my eyes watered constantly trying to get rid of its grittiness. Remembering our discussion at breakfast, I knew that this was not one of those days when schools are ordered to keep children inside for recess. *If this is a good-air day, what must the air be like on a 'stay inside bad-air' day?* I muttered to myself.

I stood on the curb near the main street trying to hail another cab and return to where Yolanda was studying. I hailed 4-5 cabs before one stopped for me. "Embajada Britanica," I said, but he didn't seem to understand my Spanish. I showed him the paper, and when he saw the address, he wagged his head yes, and I got in. As he drove, he held my crinkled piece of paper, my lifeline, in front of him in his left hand, while he steered the car with his right hand. We passed a truck stranded on the side of the road, belching black smoke as the driver tried in vain to get it into gear while cars zipped by. I tried not to breath until we got far away from the truck and its pollution. After 30 minutes of traffic jams, with two more stranded trucks and subsequent breath holding, the cab driver turned off the highway into an area that I recognized as near the British Embassy. He had found it! I paid the driver, walked across the parking lot to Yolanda's car, and planted myself on the curb beside it to wait for her.

"They were closed!" I groaned at Yolanda as she came out of the Embassy carrying her English books.

"Why are you sitting on the ground?" she asked. "You could have come inside to wait."

"Maybe the Nicaraguan Embassy people are not going to go to work anymore because the Sandinistas lost," I said, ignoring her question about why I was sitting on the curb. "I am sure all the Embassy employees are Sandinistas," I continued. "Otherwise they wouldn't have government jobs. Maybe they'll all just quit, stay home, and stop issuing visas. Maybe I should quit too and go home."

Yolanda ignored my vision of looming catastrophe. "Oh, you can try again Wednesday. I have another class then," she replied, totally at ease with dropping me off to travel by myself around Mexico City. She reassured me that an office being closed was normal. "Latin countries are slow to get things done. It will work out eventually," she promised.

"I don't know about that," I grumbled. "I probably won't be able to get a visa until April after the inauguration… it is already the second week of March now." Thoroughly dejected, I remained sitting on the curb until Yolanda opened the passenger door of the car and told me to get in. As we drove home in the car, I thought, how can I stay with Yolanda that long? I was desperate. Please God… I need a visa! NOW.

Wednesday, I repeated the trip—thirty-minute cab to the Satélite, turn into the shaded side street, and walk up the stairs to the embassy's front door. Again, the Cerrada sign was there: Closed. This time I asked the taxi driver to wait until I knew if the Nicaraguan Embassy was closed, so he could take me back to the British Embassy. I didn't want to be standing alone again at the side of the highway hailing a cab in all that traffic.

The next two weeks, the third and fourth week of March, I went both Monday and Wednesday. Same story. Will it ever be open? This is crazy, I thought. I'm supposed to be learning something, and all I am learning is how to say Satélite and to call Mexico City 'Mexico' like the residents… Come on, Embassy. Open-up. I need a visa.

On Monday April 2nd, to my surprise there was a new hand-lettered sign: Abierta. The Embassy was open! I waved off the waiting taxi and gingerly pushed open the heavy wooden front door. Inside the door, I found a young, presumably Nicaraguan woman standing beside a large brown wooden desk located about three feet to the right of the door. She was dressed in a black straight skirt that fell just below her knees, a soft white silk blouse dotted with small colorful flowers, and brown leather sandals. She had pulled her long black wavy hair back in a ponytail to control it while she worked.

She smiled as I came through the door. "Hello, I'm Andrea Fuentes. How may I help you?" she said in slightly accented English as she walked around and sat down behind the desk.

"I need a visitor's visa to go to Nicaragua to study the child welfare system," I told her in English. Behind her, hanging on a light beige wall typical of government offices, were large colored portraits of Daniel Ortega and Sergio Ramirez, the President and Vice-President of Nicaragua who had just been defeated in the election five weeks before.

"Fill out this form now and come back in a couple of days," she pleasantly told me in English, as she began looking through the appointment book on her desk.

Really, I thought, after all these months of drama it comes down to filling out a form and coming back in a few days? But smiling at her I said only, "Thank you so much. What day should I come back?"

"Can you come back tomorrow? I can have the visa for you by then," she assured me.

I could feel the relief rush through me, as I realized I would be in Nicaragua in a few days. As there were no other visitors to the Embassy, we began talking about the election. Andrea told me she was upset about the loss. "After the Inauguration, I will lose my job here in Mexico and will return to Managua or to Estelí where my family lives." As we commiserated about all the changes, I marveled how she could still be so friendly and nice amid such personal losses. But I have found over the years that Nicaraguan women are always nice, preternaturally nice.

I hailed a cab by the highway with no trouble, somewhat oblivious this time to the whizzing cars, and arrived back at the British Embassy before Yolanda's class got dismissed. Instead of sitting moping on the curb, I went into the Education section of the British Embassy searching for her, slipped into the back of her classroom and, after she spotted me, gleefully made gestures at her while mouthing, "I got it. I got it." After class I told her, "Only one more trip telling a taxi driver to find the Satélite, and I am off to Managua!"

On Wednesday April 4, 1990, after a smooth ride from Mexico City to Managua on a Continental flight, I arrived just after sunset at the Cesar Augusto Sandino International Airport, which at that time was small, about the size of a regional airport in the Midwest of the U.S. There were no gates. After landing, passengers had to walk down the stairs and across the tarmac to reach the door of the airport building, where immigration officers were waiting to check our visas.

When I reached the door of the plane, the air hit me like a blast furnace. Why is the air so hot? I wondered, somewhat alarmed that there might be a fire.

As I stood in the doorway of the plane on top of the stairs leading to the tarmac, I thought, maybe the hot air is from the engines. I looked to my left to see if the jet engine was the source of the heat. But, the blades of the engine were still. The hot air continued coming at us from all directions.

"It was 80 degrees in Mexico when we left. This feels like it is over 100," I said to the passenger behind me, who was muttering "Oh my God" out loud to herself as we walked down the stairs of the plane toward the tarmac. Somehow I had failed to think about Mexico City being cooler because of its altitude. It is in the Central Highlands of Mexico, at about 7,350 feet elevation (over 2,000 ft. higher than Denver), while Managua is situated at sea level. In addition, March and April are the killer months for heat in Nicaragua, which I was about to find out. I had landed in the hottest month at the hottest spot in Nicaragua, and the temperature was indeed over 100. The large round thermometer on the wall as we entered the airport building read 40 C (103 F).

As I stood in line inside the building waiting to get through immigration, sweat began dripping from my forehead into my eyes, stinging them and making it hard to see. I put my hand up to my head and realized my hair was dripping wet as if I had just gotten out of a shower. Sweat was dripping off the end of my nose. I was sweating like a pig!

The airport was not air-conditioned, and it was filled with a sea of warm bodies, waiting for passengers to emerge from immigration, find their baggage, and go through customs. The pungent smell of sweat and cigarette smoke was everywhere. After getting through immigration, I walked over to where large cardboard boxes and suitcases tied together with belts were coming through a hole in the wall. After I retrieved my two large suitcases, I headed to customs, dragging the suitcases behind me on their wheels.

As I emerged out of customs into the room filled with

expectant relatives, I saw people waving furiously in my direction. But they were trying to get the attention of the people coming behind me. I looked around for Sharon. How am I ever going to recognize her in this mob? I thought. Suddenly I saw a sign with my name on it being held high by a young man, so I headed in the direction of two American-looking 20-somethings dressed in cut-off jeans and tee-shirts holding the handmade sign. They towered over the sea of Nicaraguan families and street children that surrounded them in the waiting area. At last, I had found Sharon Lawlor and her colleague, Alex Stevenson, my contacts from Friends of Nicaragua, although I was not very happy to meet them. I was still annoyed at all the trouble they had caused me. Since they didn't get me a work visa, as promised, I was forced to go to Mexico, where there was a Nicaraguan Embassy, to seek out a visitor's visa on my own.

Sharon's first words of greeting were, "Are you Ann? ......you need to know that we are leaving Nicaragua next week."

Alex, who was standing to her left, still holding the sign above his head, chimed in, "Nicaragua is not safe now for Americans."

I was speechless. As we dragged the two suitcases toward the exit and wended our way through the crowd of street children begging for money and offering gifts of animals made from palm fronds, Sharon warned me, "You should never leave the house."

"It's not safe," Alex commented. As I stared blankly at him, he continued, "We are packing already and leaving next Tuesday."

I couldn't believe it! First you don't get me a visa, and now you're abandoning me, I snarled silently to myself, totally furious. This is so paranoid and over the top. Here I am in a foreign country barely understanding the language, and now my contacts are pulling out because they are afraid... afraid of what... the Sandinistas that they came to help? If I hadn't been so hot and tired, I would have sworn at them. As it was, I stewed in silence in the backseat of Alex's truck.

I'll bet they came here thinking they were going to save the world and help the Sandinistas bring about a great Revolution, I assumed, as I stared at the back of the heads of these young 'revolutionaries' cowering before the shock of having lost an election. Grow Up! I wanted to yell at them. You have projects helping people in Managua… and you are abandoning them because you are scared the defeated Sandinistas won't like you… because your government helped Doña Violeta Chamorro defeat them and win the presidential election.

By now, I was getting mad thinking about the single mothers that Sharon was abandoning, and God knows what or whom Alex was abandoning to fend for himself.

Maybe they didn't come to 'help the people,' as Sharon was fond of claiming when we discussed Nicaragua over the phone… getting more cynical by the moment. Maybe they came to meet their own needs to be important by supporting a party and a government brought about by revolution in 1979… and now their dream is over with the loss of an election… Babies! Playing at Revolution! Puffing yourselves up thinking you are changing the world, when all you are doing is using poor people to make yourselves feel good… and abandoning them when you fear it might be dangerous. Go home crying to your mothers if you're scared. But don't think I am going to cower in my room and never leave the house, because the Sandinistas lost the election. I came for the children, not for the government.

"We have put you in the Casa San Juan," Sharon told me, as we traveled on the Carretera Norte with the two suitcases in the back of the truck for a 30-minute ride across Managua. Although it was dark at 6:30 P.M., many people were walking along the street or sitting in front of what looked like shacks, lighted only by TV screens visible through the open doors. "It is a guest house for foreign visitors near the Jesuit-run University of Central America," Sharon continued. After we passed the front of the campus of the UCA, Alex turned left and drove up a curving street for two blocks to a large white house on the right with a sign in front that read, Casa San Juan.

We were greeted at the door by Francisco Mejia (called Don Fran by everyone) and his wife Anita, the owners of the Casa San Juan. His daughter, Marta, was across the room sitting in a rocking chair. When we entered, she stood up and came over to greet us warmly. There didn't appear to be anyone else, including other guests, living there.

Don Francisco Mejia was a small friendly 65-year-old Nicaraguan man about 5'3" with grey thinning hair. He had owned the Casa for nearly 10 years and ran it as a guest house for international visitors. He would not rent to Nicaraguans. When he was not painting, or fixing up cracks in the walls, he loved to write poetry.

Doña Anita was Don Fran's second wife. Marta's mother had died years before. Doña Anita was taller than Don Fran, and heavier. She was also younger, in her mid-50s, and very energetic. Truthfully, it was Doña Anita, rather than Don Fran, that kept the house in shape and running smoothly.

Marta Mejia, age 35, was one of 11 children of Don Fran (I never did figure who belonged to which mother) and was a trained accountant. A younger brother was a pediatric resident at the children's hospital, Velez Paiz. Marta managed all the books for the Casa San Juan, but lived a mile or more away in the Colonia Centro America with her two-year-old son, Marcelo, her teenage maid, Orquidia, and a teenage niece, Carolina.

Marta showed Sharon and me where I would be staying in a bedroom just off the living room to the right. It was small, about 8' x 8', with a single bed, a table and chair, plus a closet. There was no dresser, so I would be living out of my suitcases. The bed had a single pillow with a white pillowcase, a white bottom sheet, and a crisp white top sheet, ironed, folded, and placed at the bottom of the bed like an extra blanket. There were no blankets or a spread. With no air conditioning, this room is going to be hot, I realized.

While the room was sparse, it was very clean with fresh white paint on its cement block walls, topped by a reddish brown 6" wide paint trim where the wall met the ceiling. The ceiling of the room, which was also the roof of the house, was made of corrugated tin. From the ceiling, a small lamp with a single light bulb hung over the table and could be turned on and off by a switch just inside the door. The floor was made of 12-inch square maroon tiles, and down one step from the bedroom was my private bathroom with a toilet, sink, and shower. There was no bathtub.

A large mirror hung over the sink and, as we toured, I caught sight of myself out of the corner of my eye. "God help us, I look like I went swimming in salt water and rolled in the dirt like a dog. I am such a mess!" I commented in English to Marta, who made no response. Maybe she doesn't understand English, I thought.

My black hair was wet and matted to my head in odd looking waves, and all the lines and wrinkles on my face were filled with dirt, which made them more noticeable.

I resembled a 90-year-old woman who had been working in the garden. Oh dear God, I need a shower, I said to myself, as I followed Marta and Sharon up the one step to the bedroom and then into the living room where we joined Alex and Don Fran. Doña Anita had gone to sit on the front porch.

Marta showed us the living room where there were rocking chairs in three corners of the room with small tables beside them. The walls were all painted white, like my bedroom, and the floor was made of the same 12-inch-square tiles of mottled maroon colors. There were no rugs. A green string hammock was hung, using large metal hooks, between the front wall of the living room and a cement 4"x4" post next to the dining room, that was holding up the roof as well as the hammock. Here, rolled into the hammock, Don Fran could rest and watch the large TV that was on a table near the front door. The dining room consisted of a very large heavy oak table with eight straight-back wooden chairs, four on each side. Along the wall to the left was a large wooden credenza covered with little figurines, as well as plates and cups. Along the wall to the right was a large deep refrigerator.

It contained bottles of Coke and other brands of pop made in Mexico, like Rosita. If you wanted to buy a soft drink, you had to lean over the edge of the refrigerator to haul it out.

As Marta finished giving us the tour, Sharon asked me, "Is this going to be OK for you?"

I assured her it was fine, thinking what would you do if I said no?

"We will pick you up tomorrow at 8:00 a.m. to go to a school in the barrio near Siete-Sur," Alex told me as they headed toward the door.

"OK," I said, wondering why a school. Maybe they don't know what 'child welfare' means and what I am in Nicaragua to do. They seem to think I want to work with children in a school. I guess I'll find out tomorrow, I thought as I waved good-bye to them, knowing I was too tired and fed up to discuss anything more with them that night.

After Sharon and Alex left, Marta turned to me and asked slowly and clearly, "Te gustaría sentarte afuera?" (Would you like to sit outside?) "Hace mucho calor, y hay temblores en calor como este." (It is very hot and there are temblores in heat like this).

I could understand most of the Spanish words she used, because she spoke slowly. However, I guessed that the word temblores meant thunderstorms. "No Gracias, tengo que desempacar" (No thanks, I have to unpack), I told her, wondering why she and the others were all sitting outdoors waiting for a thunderstorm. Won't they all get wet out there? I asked myself, confused about the invitation. With this heat, the thunderstorm is going to be a doozy!

I left to unpack my clothes, set up my computer, and find the towels I had packed, so I could take a shower and not continue to look like something the cat dragged in.

After my shower, I should go talk to Don Fran, Doña Anita, and Marta out on the front porch and try to make friends, I told myself, as I took out the book of directions for using the new little computer I had brought with me, and turned it on.

Unbeknownst to me, there had been a small earthquake off shore ten minutes before we landed in Managua. It had not done any damage, but it had people on edge. At that time, I was not aware that many people in Nicaragua believed that earthquakes were caused by hot weather, despite their 'big one' happening on December 23, 1972, one of the coolest days of the year. The idea that hot weather could cause earthquakes, which happen deep underground, didn't compute for me. It never occurred to me that temblor meant anything other than a thunderstorm, although I did wonder why anyone would invite me to go sit outside to wait for the rain to start.

Sitting on the side of my bed in my hot and stuffy bedroom, reading the directions about how to save files on the new computer, I became aware of the tile floor moving in waves like the bottom of a rubber raft. The computer! I thought. As I stood holding onto the bed and then the chair, trying to walk across the rolling undulating floor to turn off the computer, I heard loud screaming.

I quickly looked to the right through the open door of my bedroom and saw two totally naked teenage girls run by screaming while trying to wrap themselves in sheets, which flew out behind them like sails.

"Welcome to Nicaragua!" I said laughing, then realized in a flash, I need to get out of here. Temblor means earthquake, not thunderstorm. Run outside. I raced out of my bedroom, through the living room and out the front door to join the others. Everyone was on the porch, including the two girls, by now wrapped in their white sheets. After ten to fifteen minutes, Doña Anita decided the earthquake was over, so I went back to my room.

It is very hot, dry, and dusty in Nicaragua in April. After my cold shower, which was surprisingly refreshing, I could not sleep, even with a large oscillating electric fan blowing hot air over me. Finally, I soaked the big green beach towel that I had brought with me in the sink, stripped naked, and slept with the fan blowing over the wet towel which covered me from head to toe. I always knew I would use my physics training someday, I thought, as I drifted off to sleep.

Getting up to go to the bathroom during the night I forgot there was a step down from my room to the bathroom. I fell and caught the little toe on my right foot on the cement stair. Now what? I moaned sitting naked in the dark on the bathroom floor as I reached for the throbbing toe. From the way it felt I knew it was broken. Maybe I can tape it to the other toes in the morning and wait for it to heal. You can't put a cast on a broken toe! But what if I can't walk…

# Chapter 6

# Finding a Project

Early Thursday morning as light was just breaking, I woke to the throbbing pain of my toe and the sound of the fan blowing over the green bath towel, now dry, that covered my naked body. In the distance, I could hear roosters crowing. Why are there roosters in the city? I moaned groggily as I sat up. I hadn't seen any farms on my way to the UCA campus the night before. But then I remembered, there always seem to be roosters in Nicaragua, no matter where you are.

I stepped gingerly out of bed onto my right foot, grimaced as pain shot up my leg, and started dragging wrinkled clothes out of my suitcase. I finally found a Band-Aid and taped my little toe to its neighbor, hoping that the Band-Aid would keep it still, so it would stop throbbing. I put on a pair of black Bermuda shorts and a dark purple t-shirt that read 'Pastors for Peace' in English on the front, along with red and yellow graphic designs. Maybe I should wear white, I thought, remembering that dark colors retain heat. Forget it. No matter what color you wear today, you are going to roast.

As I tried to slip my right foot, with Band-Aid attached, into a sneaker, I realized that my toe was too swollen to fit comfortably into a shoe. I hope I can get sandals on over this toe, I thought as I searched through my suitcase for my white sandals.

By loosening the straps, I widened the sandal, so my sore toe could fit in unmolested. It is going to be difficult to walk, I thought, as pain streaked up my leg at every step, even with the Band-Aid holding the toe firmly in place.

As I limped into the dining room, I noticed that Don Fran and Doña Anita, the owners of the Casa San Juan, were sitting at the table, already finishing up their breakfasts. One of the two teenagers that had flown by my doorway stark naked the night before was clearing the table. The other was mopping the living room floor with a string mop soaked in some strong disinfectant. They must be the Casa's maids, I thought. But I wonder if they are related to Don Fran? They are awfully young to be working, and they seem to live here.

When I sat down to eat breakfast, Doña Anita asked if I would like gallopinto. I had no idea what that was, but guessed it had something to do with a rooster, since gallo means rooster. She also asked how I would like my eggs, to which I replied "revuelto" (scrambled), the only egg word I knew in Spanish. What I ended up with was a mixture of rice and beans and scrambled eggs and a cup of coffee made with instant Presto. I found out later from Don Fran that gallopinto literally means 'painted rooster,' and the mixture of rice and beans, ubiquitous in Nicaragua at all meals, looks like the mottled breast feathers of a rooster.

I had barely finished eating when Sharon and Alex arrived to take me to the work site that they had arranged for me.

We drove along the main highway away from the UCA campus and toward the volcano with the large FSLN letters looming over the western edge of the city, reminding everyone that the Frente Sandinista de la Liberación de Nicaragua (i.e., the Sandinistas), was still the political party in control of the government. "Do you think those letters will remain after the new government takes over?" I asked them. They both just shrugged.

Suddenly we turned right onto a dirt road and entered a poor barrio, made up of a mixture of cardboard houses and small cement block houses with tin roofs. Alex drove carefully along the narrow road, a dirt path really, until we got to a cement block building with a tin roof. The roof extended about two feet beyond the walls to provide protection during the rainy season, and there was about four feet of space between the bottom of the roof and the top of the walls, which were only four feet high. The roof was supported by beams of cinder block every six feet that extended up beyond the walls. It looked like in the past the structure might have been painted blue, because there were flecks of blue paint here and there on the outside wall. But from a distance it appeared dirty gray.

"This is a public school," Alex explained. "They have some children here that won't stay in their classroom, and the teachers need someone to work with them."

"Maybe this is someplace you can work," Sharon said hopefully, as I quickly realized she thought I wanted to work teaching children. She had no inkling that child welfare meant working with families of children that had been abused or neglected and with children living in out-of-home care.

I was so accustomed to using the term "child welfare" with my social work students in Nebraska, that I had forgotten that most people don't know what the term means. Standing in the dirt outside an elementary school in Managua, I finally realized that I had totally neglected to explain to Sharon what, exactly, child welfare involved, and she had guessed 'teaching.' It is not only English to Spanish communication that can get derailed, I thought. I had managed to derail English to English communication by using jargon.

"I am not a special education teacher," I told her. "But I will give it a try."

"We'll come back to get you this afternoon at 5:00, after the afternoon classes get out," Sharon assured me as she and Alex left me at the school for the day.

What a day! Children who couldn't sit still in their assigned classrooms, which each had 60 other children and no books, simply wandered around the classrooms and in the yard. The head teacher, Señora Marta Lorena Reyes Munguia, led me to a small 8' by 11' room with a single metal chair placed in the middle. The seat and backrest of the chair were made from wooden slats attached to a metal frame. There was no other furniture in the room. The floor was made of cement, as were the low walls. The walls were not painted any color, but looked the color of the ground outside.

Standing, I could see out into the schoolyard through the opening between the wall and the roof; there was only dirt swirling around in small circles with the wind, and a dog, so thin that all its bones were visible.

Sitting down on the hard wooden-slat chair, all I could see were the dirty grey walls and the tin roof. The only color in the room was my purple t-shirt.

The first child the head teacher brought in for me to teach was Edgar, a boy I guessed was about 8 years old, although age is hard to determine, because many of the children are smaller than their age because of malnutrition. The instructor had no curriculum or lesson that she wanted me to teach. Her only comment as she left him with me was, "He won't sit in his chair in the classroom."

"Edgar," I said. "Ven aqui," (come here) but Edgar continued to wander aimlessly around the room where I was sitting. He was dressed in navy blue pants, a white shirt, and black leather shoes; the typical Nicaraguan school uniform. I tried to talk to him, but he either couldn't understand my words or he was living in a dream world of his own. This kid has something wrong with him, I thought to myself. He is either cognitively delayed or has a mental health disability. For half an hour, I tried to at least make eye contact with him, but nothing worked. He just wandered, not saying anything, and not paying attention to me.

Suddenly, another boy, also in a school uniform and led by a frustrated teacher, came into the room yelling and trying to pull away from her. She said something to me rapidly in Spanish, which I interpreted, more from her tone than from her words, as, "See if you can do something with him. His name is Ricardo," and left him there. He sat down on the floor in the corner, wrapped his arms around his knees, and proceeded to rock back and forth. Edgar took no notice of him.

I tried to make eye contact with Ricardo, but he too was clearly in another world. He acted like he was autistic, or perhaps had been traumatized. He wanted nothing to do with me.

I wonder if he lived somewhere near the fighting? I thought, trying to make sense of the child I was looking at. There are still killings by the Contras, especially in the north near the Honduran border… maybe he saw his father murdered… maybe he and his family are new to Managua… maybe… "

Ricardo looked very frightened of me. When I walked over toward where he was rocking and humming on the floor, he ducked his head onto his knees. How am I supposed to teach these children reading, writing, and arithmetic if they cannot function? These kids are not even here mentally… this is way beyond me! I thought, in despair of even making human contact with them. What have I gotten myself into?

I decided I would need to find out, from the head teacher or from the classroom teachers, what the story was on each of these children before I could even begin to work with them. I clearly wasn't helping anyone to learn that day.

Later Señora Reyes, the head teacher, came to get the two boys and brought me a tiny little girl, Abigail, who, although she looked about 3, must have been about 6 or 7-years-old, because both of her front teeth were missing, and one permanent tooth was beginning to come in.

After looking me over and sizing me up from the safety of the corner of the room, she began to talk to me, although I had trouble following what she said. I asked her what her name was, and was startled to get four names as the response. How can she have four names? I thought and asked her again what her name was. Again, she answered with four names. Later I would find that almost all children have four names in Nicaragua: first name, middle name, father's surname, mother's surname. And they regularly recited all four of them!

All day long, the head teacher would bring me children that needed special help. And all day long I failed to teach them anything. With each passing hour, I got more and more frustrated. I also got hungry, since I had not brought anything for lunch. There was nowhere to go to get food. Since Sharon and Alex wouldn't be back until 5 p.m., I was trapped.

Several of the children assigned to me were obviously cognitively delayed. They looked like the children I had worked with in the 1970s at the Lancaster Office of Mental Retardation. Several were perhaps only learning disabled, but many acted like they had mental health or behavioral health problems. With no curricula, no books, and no training in special education, I couldn't help them, even if they understood my Spanish. Clearly this school isn't going to work as a place to study the child welfare system of Nicaragua.

After the children left for the day, Señora Reyes, the principal, announced that we would have a teacher's meeting. "Oh, thank God, I thought, I can get some advice on how to handle these particular children. The dozen or so teachers filed into the teachers' room and sat on hard wooden chairs around a large wooden table that nearly filled the entire space. Most of the teachers were young women in their early twenties, although there were two equally young male teachers. Señora Reyes was older, perhaps 40. These teachers have degrees in education," I reassured myself. "They will have some suggestions about how to help Edgar, Ricardo, Abigail, and the others.

I took out a pen and a miniature notebook that I had in my small backpack, ready to take notes of their suggestions. However,

I quickly found that the teachers' meeting was not for going over specific children or teaching strategies. Rather, it was a daily self-accusation, done by the teachers one by one, about how they had failed that day to live up to the ideals of the Revolution. I sat at the table watching wide-eyed as these young teachers, one after another, accused themselves of various transgressions, like not acting in the Sandinista way (whatever that might mean) and not following the teachings of the Revolution. As they proceeded around the table, one after the other, accusing themselves of failure as Sandinista revolutionaries, the phrase that popped into my mind was, mind control. I sat there, my jaw dropping in amazement, fascinated, and at the same time, appalled and somewhat frightened.

I'll be damned! I thought.

All the teachers were fervent Sandinistas trying to be perfect revolutionaries. They continued to go around the circle, each one telling about how, that day, she had not lived up to the Sandinista ideology. There was nothing about the children, their needs, or how to help them. It was all about the teachers' own revolutionary fervor. When it came my turn, they asked me if I would like to confess my failures to implement Sandinista revolutionary ideology that day.

I thought to myself, this is so abnormal. But out loud I said, "No, my Spanish is too poor." The whole exercise made me very anxious, and I could feel adrenaline surging through my body. This was a political system I didn't understand and which obviously frightened me. Why are they acting like this, I thought? It is so weird. Is there some way I can quietly leave the room and get out of here? In addition to the weirdness, I knew I didn't have the talent to function as a teacher. I need to get out of here… now! I told myself, hoping that Sharon or Alex would soon appear to rescue me.

The experience of group revolutionary fervor reminded me of my 1986 visit to Managua, and Mercedes, the child welfare leader we had visited. She had seemed so blind to the reality in front of us. She spouted off ideology and the rightness of the Sandinista way, while the children in front of us were behaving very strangely and were not developing normally.

It had seemed weird to me then that ideology could so strongly affect her ability to observe reality. But it also made me wonder if the reality I thought I saw in front of me, was perhaps not true.

Maybe everything I think I see is also being affected by my own ideology, I pondered uneasily, as I turned that idea over and over in my mind. What am I choosing to look at? What am I ignoring? What is truly real? The whole experience was making me crazy.

The only other time I had heard of something resembling this self-accusation technique was when one of the Oblate priests at Sacred Heart Church in Lincoln told me, "In seminary every night at dinner we were required to accuse ourselves publicly of not totally living up to Catholic doctrine or morals that day. We would make up sins to accuse ourselves of in front of our classmates. 'I didn't brush my teeth correctly today, Father.' 'I didn't make a hit in the baseball game.' It was a big joke."

But to these teachers, it was no joke. They were seriously trying to see the world and act as the Sandinista socialist doctrine prescribed. Their true-belief truly frightened me.

By the time Sharon came to pick me up from the school, I was in a funk, with a pounding toe and a pounding headache that was rapidly turning into a migraine. I told her, "This is not going to work. I was in Nicaragua in 1986 and visited orphanages. I know they have them. Find me an orphanage or a children's home. I need to work there, not here in this crazy school."

It was clear Sharon didn't know much about how Nicaragua cared for its abandoned children. I told her, "Back in 1986, there was an orphanage for babies and toddlers that I visited in San Marcos, and there was another government orphanage for older children somewhere here in Managua. See if you can find that one."

Sharon left me at the Casa San Juan to nurse my headache and went off in search of a better place for me to work. I took two aspirin, removed all my sweaty clothes, and went to bed. My head pounded. My toe pounded. It was hot. As I lay there naked with the fan blowing on the wet towel I had laid over me again, all I could think about were the young teachers going around the table confessing their shortcomings and failures as revolutionaries. What the hell was all that about? Doesn't anyone care about the kids? I don't understand this country at all.

The next day I experienced my first taste of what life was like for ordinary Nicaraguans. "Everyone in Nicaragua writes poetry," Don Fran boasted, as he took delight in my reading his poems out loud. He had written poetry about Rubén Dario and laughed when I pronounced the famous writer's name like I was reading English. "No, no," Don Fran said. "It is pronounced roo-BEN dar-EE-o." All I could think of was my efforts in Mexico to pronounce Satélite and not say satellite. Spanish words that are very close to English words seem to be my downfall.

"Would you like to ride with me today to Granada?" Don Fran asked. "I have to visit some people."

I was thrilled and accepted immediately. Before we left, he and I struggled to lift a large 100-pound bag of rice and a similar bag of dried beans into the back seat of his little Toyota. Our first stop was to visit an old woman, Doña Melba, who lived in a tiny 8' by 8' house with a dirt floor.

As soon as we arrived, a short overweight old woman limped out on her bare feet and invited us to come into the house. It was dark and hot inside and smelled of burnt wood. There were no windows. Only the light streaming in from the open front door illuminated the room. There didn't appear to be any electric lamps. The interior was further darkened by walls covered with soot from the cooking done inside the house.

Don Fran and Doña Melba talked while I looked around, trying not to gawk, as my eyes gradually became adjusted to the low light. The old woman seemed sick, with swollen discolored legs. She was shorter than five feet in height, even if she could stand up straight, and was probably in her mid-60s. Her skin was dark, the color and texture of leather, and her large rough hands looked like she had spent a lifetime working with them. Her legs and feet were very swollen with purple spots all over them, and she appeared to have trouble walking more than a few steps. Looking at her feet I could see years of callouses on the bottoms and realized she had likely gone barefoot for most of her life, despite initially assuming she was barefoot, because her feet were so swollen that they couldn't fit into shoes.

As my eyes became more adjusted to the dark, I looked around the room trying to figure out how she lived in such a small space. There was not much in the house except the chairs we were sitting on, a table, a few dishes. I couldn't see a bed. Maybe it is behind that blanket hanging there, I guessed.

It was the dirt floor though that startled me. This floor is as solid and hard as concrete, I said to myself as I rubbed my foot against the rock-like dirt floor, hoping Don Fran or Doña Melba wouldn't notice.

Something in a corner of the room caught my eye. Oh my God, she has a broom made from a branch of a tree, its leaves still attached, I realized. In 1986, I had seen such brooms from a distance, but here was one up close in a house. She must have cut the branch off with a machete.

Doña Melba complained about her swollen legs and feet. Don Fran looked solicitously at them as if he were a doctor examining a patient, gave her medical advice, and pressed a little money into her hand to buy some medicines. Then we were off.

When we got to Granada we headed to the warehouse area and pulled up in front of what looked like an abandoned warehouse. "You stay in the car until I see if she is here," Don Fran said slowly to me in Spanish so I would understand. He banged on one of the warehouse doors. Soon a tall elegant woman,

Cristiana Bonilla, came out onto the loading dock, and we all three struggled to lift the big sacks of rice and beans onto the dock.

As I watched Doña Cristiana and Don Fran haul the bags into the warehouse, I thought, she doesn't look like the woman we just visited. This woman looks upper-class. Señora Bonilla was taller than most Nicaraguan women, and stood very erect like a queen. She had fine soft hands, not the hard-calloused hands of Doña Melba or the women I saw selling food in the street. What is she doing here? I wondered.

Maybe she owns this warehouse and Don Fran is delivering the beans and rice for her business. Inviting us to follow her, Doña Cristiana led us into the warehouse. In a corner by the large doors I saw a small khaki army cot with folding wooden legs. There were no sheets or blankets near the cot.

Must be for the night watchman, I surmised.

Later in the car, Don Fran told me that it was Señora Bonilla, the tall elegant 70-year-old woman we had just met, who slept there. He had brought the rice and beans to keep her alive. I was stunned, and felt confused and anxious. This cannot be happening, I thought. "Who is she?" How do you know her?" I asked Don Fran, trying to make sense out of what appeared to me to be an impossible situation.

As we drove back to Managua, Don Fran explained. "Señora Cristiana Bonilla was a well-known musician, a concert pianist, but her savings were wiped out by the hyperinflation of the 1980s. She has no children and doesn't know how to work as a domestic. In the 1980s the Sandinista government drafted more and more young men to serve in the army and printed more and more Córdobas to pay them. Piles of Córdobas that used to be worth thousands of dollars are now worth pennies. All her savings evaporated, so a friend of hers who owns the warehouse, lets her sleep there."

Immediately I flashed back to the discussion group at Sacred Heart Church about Latin America. We had read the book about "low intensity warfare" and how the U.S., to bring the Sandinista government to its knees, was destroying the economy in Nicaragua. By causing rampant inflation in a smaller economy, the U.S. could wipe out resources that might be used to institute policies not in accord with the U.S. government's wishes.

The U.S. apparently used the same strategy to induce the collapse of the Soviet economy. By implying that we had a workable 'Star Wars' capability, we forced the Soviets into large investments in weaponry, more than their economy could bear. The Reagan years (1981-1989) were marked by low intensity warfare, where the strength of the U.S. economy was used to destroy smaller economies. There was no need to bomb or invade. A government with a collapsed economy cannot feed, clothe, or educate its people, and eventually will not be able to pay soldiers or buy arms.

We had read about it, and discussed it at length, but here I was seeing it first-hand. An elegant cultured lady of 70 years of age was reduced to sleeping on a cot in a warehouse owned by a friend and accepting bags of rice and beans. She had no children and didn't know how to cook and clean to earn money, since she had had servants all her life. Without family, in a country without a social security system, she had no way to survive alone.

Today, when children come up to me on the street and ask for money, I tell them, "No. You need to go to school." Parents often keep them out of school to beg on the streets, cutting off their futures before they even start.

But old people sitting on the sidewalk asking for money… I always give them a few Córdobas. While I am a firm believer in development and helping people to help themselves become independent, there are times when charity is needed. The saying 'Give a man a fish, you feed him for one day; teach a man to fish and he feeds himself for a life time' goes only so far. Some old people are beyond the age of learning to fish. They just need to eat.

After searching all over Managua for an orphanage, Sharon and Alex returned the next day and took me to El Centro Rolando

Carazo, an orphanage for children, to meet someone called Marielena. "She's in charge," Sharon told me. "She'll figure out something for you to do."

Having found an orphanage as I had asked, Sharon and Alex prepared to leave me there to figure out my future without their help. "We are leaving next Tuesday. You'll be on your own, so be careful," Alex warned, as he and Sharon moved toward the door to go home to pack for their escape. "The Nicaraguans hate Americans now… they may hurt you… stay indoors," were his parting words as they abandoned me to the care of Marielena.

The hell I will. You guys are nuts, I thought. I am not cowering in the house every day waiting to be killed by a Nicaraguan who now hates Americans. What is wrong with you? In a way, I was glad to be rid of them.

Most American internationals left the country in April before the new government took over, afraid for their lives and totally depressed about the collapse of the Sandinista Revolution.

The Europeans and Canadians remained, concerned about the people they were trying to help with their NGOs. The Americans working for NGOs seemed more interested in the politics of revolution than in individual NGO projects. It was embarrassing to observe their split-and-run behavior. Maybe people will think I am a Canadian or a European, I hoped, feeling for the first time in my life embarrassment at being an American.

Despite Alex's dire warnings, I didn't believe my life was in any danger as an American. But just in case, I figured I'd better fake Irish citizenship. That would be easy, with my 100% Irish ancestry and my knowledge of Ireland from my marriage to a real Irishman. I could get away with that, I told myself. I look Irish. I speak English, and no one here can tell if my accent is Irish or American. English speakers struggling with Spanish all sound the same to them. Standing in front of the mirror in my bathroom, I practiced my new identity, "Soy Ana Coyne de Malahide, circa de Dublín. Soy Irlandesa, (I am Ann Coyne from Malahide, close to

Dublin. I am Irish)," I said over and over. As I rehearsed my new identity, I reassured myself, that'll work if I need it. I'll be fine.

As I stood alone in the office waiting for Marielena, I looked out the window and felt that the buildings looked vaguely familiar. There were little houses clustered around a courtyard, below a big hill, on a very busy street. I suddenly realized Sharon had found the right orphanage. It was the same place where the school-age kids had mauled me in 1986, rubbing their bodies up against mine in a desperate search for human touch.

Since 1986, the walls had been painted yellow, and someone had painted colorful portraits of the children on the outside walls of all the little houses. However, the children in the portraits and the ones I could see playing in the courtyard were young. Maybe I can do something worthwhile here.

"Where are the children who used to live here?" I asked Marielena, after she arrived and we had exchanged pleasantries. I told her that I had been there four years before and had seen older children.

She explained, "We had trouble with the water in San Marcos, which caused an epidemic of dysentery among the babies, so we moved the younger children here to Rolando Carazo and the older children out to a center on the outskirts of Managua called Héroes y Martires."

As we talked about what I could do at Rolando Carazo, Marielena observed, "Next week is Semana Santa. You might want to start the week after that."

I could feel the panic starting. I need to start right now, I thought. I have nothing else to do... no one can understand me... what am I going to do by myself for a week?

I told her, "No I'll start Monday. I don't have anything else to do." Thankfully, she agreed.

When I explained to Marielena that I had no idea where I was and that Sharon and Alex had left me to find my own way home, she drove me to the Casa San Juan, pointing out how close

I lived to Rolando Carazo. "Monday morning I will come get you and show you how to ride the bus," she promised.

I could feel my body relax. At last, I have found a place for my sabbatical.

## Chapter 7

## Semana Santa

Monday morning of Holy Week, April 9, 1990, bright and early at 7:00 a.m., Marielena drove to the Casa San Juan in her little Lata, a Bulgarian car driven frequently in Managua, especially by taxi drivers. "Are you ready?" she said. "I'll show you how to get to Rolando Carazo on the bus."

We walked the two blocks down the curved neighborhood street which wound in front of the Casa, past the metal fence that marked the western edge of the UCA campus, until we got to the main highway, the Carretera de la Resistencia. We crossed the six lane carretera gingerly, knowing that drivers, not pedestrians, have the right of way in Nicaragua.

"This is where you catch the bus," Marielena pointed out. A few UCA students were already at the stop. "We'll take it to Siete-Sur, and then walk up the hill to the Center." Soon an old bus came barreling down the highway toward us, belching black smoke. I wasn't sure it would stop. But it screeched to a halt in front of us, and we climbed on and gave the driver the Córdobas that Marielena had instructed me to get ready.

There was nowhere to sit, so I held on tight to the metal bar on the back of a seat, where three women were sitting, scrunched together in a seat for two.

There was a bar to hang onto above my head, but it was too high for me to reach, so with two hands, I grabbed onto the back of the seat in front of me, while my backpack remained crushed against another rider standing behind me. Marielena, hanging on for dear life to the back of another seat, pointed out public buildings along the way, as the bus drove erratically, rocking from side to side, down the long straight highway towards the volcano with the large letters FSLN on its side. "We stay on the bus until it can't go straight anymore," she instructed. "That's Siete-Sur." (Seven-South)

Not that hard, I thought. I can do this. Maybe coming to Nicaragua hasn't been such a boondoggle. Maybe these adventures are teaching me something.

When we got to El Centro Rolando Carazo, Marielena brought me into the infirmary and introduced me to Zaidy Scott, a British nurse who was spending two years in Nicaragua providing medical care to children. I never figured out how she got to Nicaragua. She didn't seem to be sponsored by any NGO in Nicaragua, but she clearly was being paid by some organization in England.

*At last, a person who speaks English!* I thought, exchanging my typical "mucho gusto" into "pleased to meet you" as I shook her hand. When Zaidy spoke, I could hear her strong British accent. "I used to live in England," I told her. "My husband was an international student from Ireland, so we had to leave the U.S. for two years because he was on a J1 visa. He worked for the Campbell Soup Company in Kings Lynn."

"That's in Norfolk, isn't it?" she responded with a definite nasal twang caused by her cleft palate. I nodded agreement.

"I think this will be a good place for you to work" said Marielena, breaking up our English getting-to-know-you ritual. "You can help Zaidy with the babies and the disabled children."

I was in heaven! "This is exactly where I want to be," I told Marielena, thanking her and feeling like I had dodged a bullet, after my disastrous experience in the school the Friday before. Here, at last, I could see how abandoned children were handled, and how the child welfare system in Nicaragua was organized.

After Marielena left, Zaidy showed me around the infirmary. It was in its own cottage, which had been President Somoza's sister's house before he was toppled by the 1979 Revolution. The infirmary consisted of three rooms; two bedrooms filled with small metal cribs side by side with babies' first names printed on a card and taped to the end of the bed, a feeding room with a little kitchen for heating baby food and bottles of milk, and a bathroom which had a small bathtub built into a shelf at table height. There was also a 6-foot square entryway by the front door with a small metal desk that Zaidy used as her office.

The cribs had been painted white years ago, but now they were showing more metal than paint. The walls were made of cement block, somewhat dingy in color, needing a good coat of paint to bring the rooms to life.

The windows were made of movable glass slats. They could be opened or closed with a twist of a metal knob.

Two large fans stood in each room and blew hot air around continuously. There were no ceilings, only the dark green/black metal roof which was visible if anyone looked up. In the feeding room, there were four handmade wooden feeding tables, painted bright blue. The tables were designed so that one *educadora* (caretaker) could sit in the middle and simultaneously feed two babies, who were positioned at either end of the table. I watched as a feeding took place; two bowls rested on the table just out of the babies' reach, full of what looked like oatmeal and a spoon. The babies seemed delighted to have the social interaction with their tablemate and the *educadora* feeding them.

I noticed that the tiny, but deep, square bath tub on the shelf in the bathroom had what looked like weeds floating in about 18" of water. "What is that grass doing in there?" I asked Zaidy.

"Oh, that's not grass. It's *manzanilla*," she explained, as she picked up a bunch of dry weeds that were resting on the table beside the little tub. "It is very good for babies' skin. It even gets rid of all the fungus infections abandoned babies tend to come in with." I silently wondered if bathing all the babies in the same water, even with the magical *manzanilla*, might spread infections, but didn't say anything.

After touring the infirmary with me, Zaidy realized I didn't know how to get lunch. "If you want to eat, you first need to buy a plastic soup bowl and something to put a drink in," she told me. "They don't have any plates or utensils here."

The search was on! Zaidy sent me across the street to the supermarket that fortunately was still open, despite it being Monday of Semana Santa. As I walked in the front door I could barely see anything. The store appeared pitch black at first, so I waited until my eyes adjusted to the light. Even then, it was spookily dark. There were no overhead lamps, so all the light was coming from outside, through the front door and a few small windows near the ceiling. The entire store smelled of the old discarded vegetables which I could see rotting on a few of the shelves. Most of the shelves were bare, no cans, no packages, no fruits or vegetables, nothing. On three or four shelves, there were scattered rotting onions or random leaves and stalks of celery. It was these rotting vegetables that gave the entire store its musty smell.

I asked the clerk where I could find a plastic cup and bowl. She didn't understand my Spanish, so I reverted to gestures. Using my hands, I demonstrated the size of the bowl I wanted and then made a drinking gesture as I held an imaginary cup. "Oh," she said, "arriba, (upstairs)" as she pointed me in the direction of stairs to the second floor.

I walked in the direction she was pointing until I came to what looked like handmade wooden stairs. They were odd wooden pieces nailed together, like a ladder and placed at an angle ending 15 feet above the first floor balancing on a ledge that I took to be the edge of the second floor. There were no hand rails. These stairs look rickety to climb on, I thought as I took my first step, hoping the stair didn't collapse under my weight.

As I climbed higher, I realized that Dermot would never be able to do this. But I didn't have his fear of heights, so I continued to climb, holding tight onto each higher stair with both hands. When I finally reached the top, and scrambled onto a firm floor, I went to look for something, anything, to hold my dinner. Tucked away in a dark corner were some plastic bowls and a few plastic cups. Oh, thank God they have them, so I can eat! I said half out-loud to myself as I grabbed a couple of each and descended the rickety stairs backwards, as if I were on a ship's ladder, holding on tight again so I wouldn't fall. As I began to climb down, I was high enough to look around the whole store. Its shelves were indeed all bare. How do people get food? I wondered shaking my head as I remembered the chock-full shelves in the supermarkets in Nebraska.

There are reasons why Semana Santa is often called Semana Playa. Everyone goes to the beach. Stores close. Restaurants shut down. Even the newspapers stop publishing from Holy Thursday until the day after Easter. And the main TV station broadcasts, over and over in a loop for four days, Charlton Heston as Moses parting the Red Sea. A Nicaraguan friend told me that some priests, in their bathing suits, say Mass on the beach on Easter Sunday morning.

The Casa San Juan served only breakfast. The first few days I lived there I would limp on my broken toe to the restaurant next door to eat dinner.

On Palm Sunday when I went next door for dinner after the Mass, I found the restaurant closed. I asked the owners, Don Fran and Doña Anita, about other restaurants, but they told me all restaurants in the entire city were closed for Holy Week. Surprisingly they didn't invite me to eat with them at night, and I didn't have enough language skill to know how to ask. Thank heavens I agreed to start working at the orphanage on Monday, I thought. It looks like that is the only place I can get food at noon during Holy Week. El Centro Rolando Carazo is going to keep me, as well as the abandoned children, from starving.

For a few days, I toughed it out, dizzy and lethargic, and went to bed hungry without any supper, but towards the end of the week I saw Senor Isidro Avalon, the man who ran the bread shop across the street, out in his yard. I asked him if, by chance, even though the bread shop was closed, did he have a loaf of bread I could buy?

He replied "Oh yes. I have one left to sell," and went into the house to retrieve what looked to me like the most delicious loaf of bread ever baked. I was so hungry!

Isidro Avalon was a pleasant man, about 40 years old, thin, short, and wiry, with balding black hair that he combed over the crown of his head. He pointed to the side yard where a well-dressed woman was watching his maid and her young daughter hanging out clothes to dry. He told me his cousin, Natalia Avalon, was staying with him. "She speaks English," he told me proudly as he called her over.

After exchanging the customary pleasantries, Natalia told me, "I grew up in Nicaragua, but now my husband and I live in the States, in Los Angeles. Our son died last year in a car crash," she said softly, as her eyes welled up with tears. "He was our only child." After I expressed my condolences, she told me with a smile, "We are adopting a little girl from here," and pointed to the girl helping the maid hang out the clothes. Somehow, Natalia had convinced her brother's maid to 'gift' her 10-year-old Yadira, the maid's youngest daughter.

Whoa, this could be trouble, I thought, as all my social work red-flags began waving, and I shifted into professional mode.

She had already legally adopted the child in a Managua court, Natalia told me, but the previous week when she went to the US Embassy to get the girl's visa after the adoption was finalized, the Consul told her she needed a letter from an American social worker that knew her. She had heard I was a social worker and asked, "Can you write a letter for me?" I struggled with the dilemma, weighing the pros and cons in my mind.

I don't know her very well and I don't know her husband at all. How can I do a home study? They clearly are trying to replace their son, not a good start for any adoption. Yadira will never live up to their expectations. They won't miss their son any less. This adoption may or may not be good for Yadira.

But… she has already been legally adopted. She thinks she is going to live in the U.S. If I don't write the letter, she won't be able to live with her legal parents. Then, what will happen to her? Talk about a conundrum. How do I get myself into these situations? I thought. All I wanted was a loaf of bread…

I finally decided to write a letter to the Consul saying, "I really don't know the adoptive mother well, but this is what she told me about her family." When Natalia returned to the U.S. Embassy the following week with Yadira and my letter, it appeared the Consul was just looking for a document to put in the file. He immediately issued an immigration visa for the child, and Yadira left Nicaragua for the U.S. with her new mother the following day. So much for the requirement of a home study…

I often wonder what happened to her. Was Yadira seen as a different child or as a replacement for the son they had lost? Did they abuse her or use her as a maid? Or did they raise her as their daughter? Was she homesick for her Nicaraguan mother? Or did she bond with her new mother? Was she able to adjust to U.S. culture? Or did she want to return to Nicaragua? There is no way to know, but I still worry.

All the newborns who came to Rolando Carazo were placed in the infirmary until they were placed for adoption with Nicaraguan families or until they got old enough to join the toddlers in the 3-year-old room. Additionally, disabled children who needed medical supervision were placed in the infirmary, to be cared for by Zaidy Scott and Yámileth Tinoco, a Nicaraguan nurse paid by the government.

All the workers at Rolando Carazo except Zaidy Scott, Heather Smith, Eduardo Carson, and now me were paid by the Nicaraguan government. Heather was a British speech therapist who also worked there in one of the cottages with 8 and 9-year-old children. Eduardo was a Canadian special education teacher who consulted with Marielena about policies. And, best of all, we four internacionalistas all spoke English! The other three also spoke excellent Spanish.

Zaidy and I walked through the infirmary that first day, after I had risked life and limb climbing like a monkey up that rickety handmade wood staircase to secure my cup and bowl from the second floor of the supermarket across the street. As we entered one room, I spotted a two-month-old baby girl, lying alone in a crib, wide awake and blankly staring up with large brown eyes at the dark ceiling. Her name was Eliadora Moreno, and she had a bilateral cleft lip and palate. Fortunately, years previously, I had seen a baby boy like this in a pediatrician's office sitting quietly on his mother's lap waiting to be seen for a regular well-baby visit.

At that time, I was totally shocked, and it took me awhile to figure out what was going on with him. As I sat in a chair opposite his mother, it looked to me like the baby had no face and that I could see into his brain. Eventually, as I sat there in the doctor's waiting room, holding my own baby son, I realized the baby had a cleft lip and palate, and that this is what babies look like before they have surgery. Years later in Nicaragua, I was no longer shocked.

I knew that although Eliadora's face was wide open and looked like a truck had hit her, she was just a normal baby who eventually would have surgery and look more ordinary. However, the sight of her alone in that infirmary crib, staring blankly at the ceiling without even a mobile overhead for stimulation, did shock me. All my experience as a mother, and my training in bonding and attachment of infants, told me that social isolation was a more serious problem for this baby than her cleft lip and palate.

"Zaidy, you can't let her just lie there in a crib all day. She needs to be attached to someone!" I said. "If she doesn't attach to someone," I continued, as if Zaidy were one of my social work students, "she will not develop normally." With that, I picked the baby up, and Eliadora became mine.

When I read her chart, there was some question about her birth date. One document said January 15th. The other said January 25th. But there were other notations in her medical record before January 25th, so Zaidy, with clipped British precision, announced, "January 15, 1990 must be her birthday," and wrote the date on her chart. In a week, she would be three-months-old.

Later that morning while Zaidy and I were tending the babies and the sick children, there was a bit of a commotion, as the door to the infirmary burst open and in walked three American graduate students and their professor, Dr. James Garbarino.

I had known Jim Garbarino when he was doing research at Boys Town. He had developed and taught the research course on child abuse for the School of Social Work where I worked. After he left Omaha, for years I taught 'Research in Child Abuse,' using his syllabus. Startled, we looked at one another and gasped in unison, "What are YOU doing here?"

Jim and his graduate students were writing a book about children of war. But now he was more concerned about getting food. All they had to eat were the pretzels and peanuts they had saved from the flight from Houston to Managua the night before.

"All the restaurants in the city are closed this week," I warned him. "It's Holy Week."

"How am I supposed to know that?" he groused, looking around at his hungry graduate students and realizing he had a real problem on his hands.

"You will only be able to get food at your hotel... if they are providing food to their guests," I told him, bitching that I too faced a food-free week.

One of his students, Sarah Donnelly, had set up an appointment to meet with an eight-year-old girl living in a foster home in Managua. She wanted to interview her, but didn't have a translator. The three translators whose names and numbers she had been given were all at the beach when she called them. In desperation, she asked if I could translate for her. I agreed to try, although I had never translated before… a case of the blind leading the blind.

We took a cab from Rolando Carazo to meet the foster mother, Señora Maria Torres, and the girl, Valeria Narvaez, at a street corner on the Carretera Masaya, located on the other side of the UCA campus from the Casa San Juan. Fortunately, the taxi driver could figure out the address from what Sarah had written down. To me, the address looked like gobbledygook, with directions that read: Start from (some building I didn't know), go 3 blocks "up" and then go 2.5 blocks "toward the lake." There were no street names or house numbers, no north or south! Not batting an eye at the strange address, the taxi driver found the street corner without incident. Valeria and her foster mother were waiting and motioned to us as we stepped out of the cab.

Valeria was adorable but looked wary of us. She was tiny for age eight. Her black wavy hair had streaks of yellow near the brittle ends and was painfully thin. However, the recent growth of hair closer to her head was soft, shiny, and totally black, which told me she was getting more protein now. Her big brown eyes looked quizzically at us, with interest but a lot of caution. Valeria's dark brown skin looked leather-like, since she spent most of her time in the sun without sun screen. Over her white panties, she wore a white cotton dress with colorful birds printed on it, although the color of the birds had faded and the top button in the back was missing. Upon her feet were pink flip-flops, but her callouses indicated that she had gone barefoot a good bit of her life.

Señora Maria Torres, her foster mother, looked to be about 50 years old with straight black hair mixed with grey, pulled back and rolled into a bun. She stood about 5'3" and was somewhat overweight. She reminded me of the women I had seen working in the market selling food. I never did figure out how she supported herself and Valeria. She clearly was quite poor, but she seemed happy to have Valeria to raise and eager to share with her what little she had.

After we seated ourselves cross-legged in a circle on the sidewalk in front of their 8' by 8' cardboard house, made of refrigerator shipping cartons, the foster mother began, "Last year Valeria was locked for several days in her tiny house with the body of her mother who had been shot by the Contras." I translated as Jim's student, Sarah, sat spellbound, taking notes, and ignoring the cars that constantly whizzed by. Señora Torres continued, "Finally, after two or three days the neighbors realized she was in there and broke open the door to rescue her."

Sarah and I looked at each other a bit sheepishly as we remembered all our fussing that morning about our lack of food. This child had been without food or water for over two days! Valeria told us about living in the North where all the fighting was, and I did my best to translate. Both Sarah and I became wide-eyed when she told us, "I hid from the Contras and looked for soldiers to help me."

I thought, Who the hell are these Contra mercenaries we are funding? They don't sound like Freedom Fighters to me!

Many apparently were ex-National Guard troops loyal to Somoza who had escaped to Honduras after the Sandinistas took over the Nicaraguan government in 1979. After asking Valeria all the questions Sarah had on her list, I asked the little girl, "Do you have any questions for us?"

Valeria smiled shyly and then asked, "Have you ever seen a washing machine?"

When I replied, "I have one in my house," it was she who grew wide-eyed.

"How does it work?" she whispered, and I proceeded to demonstrate with my hands how the machine swishes the clothes back and forth. She looked amazed. I didn't dare tell her I had a clothes dryer as well.

We left little Valeria Narvaez living in that cardboard hut on a busy street corner in Managua, with Señora Maria Torres, who was willing to raise the child for free. Valeria missed her rural town in the mountains and didn't like living on a corner of a busy street in Managua, but there she was. I often wonder what ever happened to her. She would be in her late-thirties by now, probably a mother herself. I wonder if Señora Torres lived long enough to raise her? Did Valeria ever go back to the mountain village where she was born? She was one of the thousands of orphans of the Contra War.

Dr. James Garbarino and his three graduate students returned to the US on the third day, because they couldn't get food or get interviews during Holy Week. Semana Santa is not a good week to come to Nicaragua to do work!

At Rolando Carazo, the women who took care of the children (educadoras), the women who cleaned the floors (limpiadoras), Zaidy, and I ate our lunches together in the infirmary after the babies went down for their naps. Most of the Nicaraguan women ate with their fingers, unless it was soup which they drank from their bowls. Zaidy and I used plastic forks and spoons.

Thursday, as we lined up in the cafeteria to get our lunch ladled into our plastic bowls, I realized lunch that day was a watery soup with a crab claw in it. I took it thinking, What in God's name am I going to do with this? Walking back across the playground to the infirmary it hit me. This is the only food I will get until tomorrow morning. I need to figure out how to eat it. I watched the Nicaraguan women break up their crab legs. There was no meat in them, just the shell. They chewed the shell, swallowed it, and then drank the water it was cooked in out of their bowls. I suppose it provides them some calcium, I thought. Maybe I should try to eat it. But what if the little sharp pieces stick into my stomach or intestines? Perforated intestines would be worse than hunger. For a while, I debated eating it, but finally drank only the soup, which was basically water. Not many calories here! But at least it won't kill me, I reasoned. That was the afternoon I went looking for bread from the neighbor man after I came home from Rolando Carazo.

Before I left on Thursday, Zaidy told me that Friday I would be going with the older children to a little town south of Managua where the people organized a parade on Good Friday, carrying through the streets the wooden body of Jesus in a glass sided coffin.

Friday, we traveled from Managua south toward Granada in the back of a pickup truck, eight children, another caretaker, and me bouncing along, sitting cross-legged on the metal floor for an hour. On the padded bench, that served as the pickup's front seat, three of the professional staff, who were on vacation for Holy Week, squeezed in with the driver. They were dressed in fine dresses, with perfect makeup, and high heels. These professional staff, dressed to the nines for their Good Friday outing, had no intention of sitting in the back of the pickup truck with us, as we swerved around pot holes and got covered with dust from the other pickups whizzing by.

When we arrived, the driver parked the pickup in a good spot, so we could all stand in the back of the truck to get a birds-eye view of the Good Friday procession. I quickly spotted the glass-sided coffin containing the wooden figure of the dead and bloodied Jesus coming toward us, carried on their shoulders by groups of 8-10 men on each side, straining under the weight of the large wooden coffin.

Following behind the coffin, groups of four men carried on their shoulders little girls dressed as angels and tied to stakes on top of 5' by 5' platforms. They were free to move their arms and legs, but their middles were firmly fastened to the stakes.

Some of the six little angels looked terrified to be up that high, despite being adequately secured. A similar group of six little boys, dressed as Roman Soldiers, were tied on top of rocking horses that were also attached to stakes on top of similar 5' by 5' platforms, each carried by four men.

Such a solemn religious event, I thought, until I spotted the ice cream man marching in the procession between the little angels and the soldiers on their rocking horses. For me it became a metaphor for Nicaragua, wherever two or more are gathered in My Name, there will be the ice cream man! It never failed. The ice cream man or the cotton-candy man honed in laser-like on crowds.

One of the children in the pickup with me was Roberto, the little 4-year-old Berto who had taken us on tour of San Marcos in 1986. He was now eight and still not adopted. Before I left, I had asked Suzanne Erickson and Lorraine Spencer at Adoption International, an international adoption agency in Omaha, "If Roberto is still there, please find him a home."

Holy Saturday and Easter Sunday were boring and difficult. I had only breakfast and my dwindling loaf of bread to sustain me. Since I didn't work on the weekends, I had no Rolando Carazo dinner, however meager, either day at noon. I could buy pop at the Casa San Juan, so the sugar in Fanta, Rosita, and Coke kept me from becoming dizzy and fainting with hunger. There was nothing on TV except Charlton Heston as Moses parting the Red Sea, over and over…

Will this week never end? I thought, complaining over and over to myself about hunger pains. I had never been hungry before, and it was no fun. How do poor people tolerate this? I thought.

# Chapter 8

# Transfer of Power

On April 16th, the Monday after Easter, when I took the bus to work I noticed that many young people riding the busses were dressed in army uniforms. During Holy Week, I hadn't seen any. Apparently, the Army took the week off too, I surmised.

That morning, as I was watching Zaidy check the heart and lungs of Ana and Bryan, a 4-year-old girl and an 18-month old boy, both with hydrocephalus, one of the limpiadoras ran into the infirmary screaming, "Four planes were just blown up at the airport!!"

Oh, oh! I thought with mounting fear. The inauguration of Doña Violeta as the new president is next week, only days away. Is this the beginning of a coup? Within minutes, the army installation on the hill behind Rolando Carazo, silent during Holy Week, suddenly began to buzz with activity. Helicopters hovered above the hill, making a frump-frump-frump noise with their blades and blowing trash around on the ground. I could see one of the helicopters over the Army post through the window, but I ran outside to look up when I heard deafening helicopter noise immediately above us. Two helicopters hovered only meters above the tallest trees, and the downdraft was blowing trash all over the playground of the orphanage. Fortunately, no children were outside.

My heart began to pound and feelings of anxiety spread all over my body at the sight of the helicopters. I had seen pictures that children in El Salvador had drawn of army helicopters dropping bombs on their villages and recognized that this looked very similar.

We might be at the beginning of armed conflict, I feared. Maybe the transfer of power from the Sandinistas to the UNO Coalition party of Doña Violeta is not going to be peaceful. I quickly turned to run back into the safety of the Infirmary, and as I turned, I could see ten or more women running out the front door of the main building and down the steps toward the street. I immediately realized that many of the caretakers and cleaning ladies at the Center had abandoned their posts and were flying out the front gate and running home.

What do they know that I don't know? I thought, as fear began to roll around in my stomach and caused my breath to catch in my throat. What is going to happen? Is it dangerous here near the Army post? Is there going to be fighting? Will we get hurt?

Zaidy and I walked around to make sure all the children in the Infirmary had been fed and had diapers changed; we checked that there were adults in each of the other cottages. I soon began to get angry at the educadoras. "How can they just run away and abandon these children?" I asked Zaidy in full mother-superior judgmental mode.

Zaidy just shrugged. "Nothing takes precedent over their own families," she said. "In this culture, family comes first, not work."

Later that afternoon, as we were trying to make do with half the usual staff, the music being played by the radio station was interrupted mid-song by a man's deep bass voice saying, "The government announced this afternoon that the explosion this morning at the airport was an accident, caused by a spark."

No one, of course, believed that four small planes had been blown up by one spark… by accident. But the government was evidently eager to cover up what had happened. The Toma de Posesión, (literally 'the Taking of Possession') referred to in English as 'The Presidential Inauguration,' would go on as planned it seemed.

"Maybe there will not be a coup after all," I said hopefully to Zaidy as we settled back into the rhythm of caring for the children in the Infirmary, and searching through the medical records for children with disabilities who needed adoptive homes. Developmentally disabled kids will not be adopted here, I realized, beginning to get a clearer picture of Nicaragua's child welfare system. Even normal infants are not adopted if they are over one-month-old.

By the middle of April, Managua had begun to fill up with dignitaries and reporters who were coming for the Toma de Posesión, which would be held in the baseball stadium Wednesday morning, April 25th. An American man, a reporter with a large city newspaper who was on assignment, and an American woman who had an interest in the Sandinistas, showed up April 24th to stay at the Casa San Juan.

The reporter, Sean Walsh, was in his mid 30s, with light brown thinning hair and brown eyes. He stood about 5' 9" tall and was a little overweight, but not fat. Sally McCormick, who owned a small store in a little town near Syracuse, N.Y., was in her early 30s, slim and as tall as Sean, with dark brown, almost black, long hair and blue eyes. She had come down on a whim to see the country before the Sandinistas were out of power.

They had not known one another before arriving at the Casa San Juan, our little hotel close to the University of Central America where I was the only guest. Sean had press credentials, but Sally and I had no tickets to the big event, only hope.

"Do you think we can get in?" I asked Sean.

"It was pretty easy to get these credentials at the Olof Palme Convention Center," he said. "They didn't ask for any identification. I just said I was a reporter and they gave them to me."

"Do you think if I strapped two cameras around my neck I could convince them I am a press photographer?" I asked, thinking the inauguration would be quite a show.

"We can't lose by trying," he replied, and then being hungry suggested, "Let's go to the Salvadoran restaurant near the Hotel Intercontinental for dinner tonight."

The next morning, the day of the Toma, I draped both cameras around my neck, and we headed off to the Convention Center to get press passes for Sally and me. There were no busses running, so we thumbed a ride part way in the back of a pickup.

When we got to the Convention Center it was closed. A guard told us, "Go over to the Stadium."

At the Stadium, I approached a guard, who looked like a high school student, and announced loudly in English, "I don't speak Spanish. I'm from the press and I just arrived. I need to get in."

The young man had no clue what this 53-year-old American woman overloaded with cameras was saying to him in English… and my companions didn't let a Spanish word escape from their lips. They just stood there looking blank, showing Sean's press pass, when the guard tried to talk to them in Spanish. As the young man argued with me, I kept saying over and over in English, "I am from the press. I need to go in. I am from the press…"

Frustrated that none of us could understand him, the guard let the three of us into the VIP section to sit with Jean Kirkpatrick, Henry Hyde, and other Republican dignitaries who had flown down with the Vice-President on Airforce Two for the presidential inauguration of Doña Violeta. Vice-President Dan Quale and his wife sat with his translator in a box on the first base side, totally in the sun… in April… the hottest month of the year. We, fortunately, were in the grandstand under cover. We had the best seats in the house.

Looking toward the outfield, we realized that people dressed in blue and white and waving blue and white Nicaraguan flags were located on the first base and right field side. Those dressed in red and black and waving the red and black Sandinista flags sat on the third base side and in left field. There was a barrier in center field between the two sides made up of soldiers.

The atmosphere crackled with excitement… mixed with some fear. What will happen if the two groups come to blows? Will there be a riot? I looked over at Jean Kirkpatrick. She was dressed all in red. Someone had neglected to tell her that blue and white were the Doña Violeta colors, and she ended up dressed like a Sandinista.

I chuckled and poked Sally, "Look at Jean Kirkpatrick. Someone in the protocol office didn't tell her the color-of-the-day."

Soon Doña Violeta's pope mobile, basically a white pickup truck, came out of the bullpen in left center field with Doña Violeta, smartly outfitted in a white linen suit, standing erect in the truck bed behind the cab and holding onto a metal bar. Daniel Ortega stood beside her with the presidential sash hanging diagonally across his chest. Running along both sides of the truck for security were eight young soldiers, as the small truck made its way slowly to home plate along the third base line.

Suddenly red and black clad partisans in the stands on the third base side started throwing sealed plastic bags filled with water at the incoming and outgoing presidents. The soldiers jumped like basketball players to deflect each water balloon, getting soaked in the process. Throw, jump, splash… throw, jump, splash… But no water reached either of the presidents. Only the soldiers got soaked.

A rumor started that it was not water they were throwing but bags of urine. Men from the blue and white right field stands tried to run through the center field stands to get to the people along the third base line who were throwing the bags of liquid.

It looked like a riot in the making, but the soldiers blockaded the center field bleachers and kept the Doña Violeta partisans out of the Sandinista areas. By the time the two presidents got to home plate, things had quieted down.

Daniel Ortega passed the sash to Doña Violeta. Cardinal Obando y Bravo droned on interminably, prompting Sean to remark as if writing a press release, "The first aggressive act of the new government toward the people of Nicaragua was to turn the Cardinal loose."

When we sensed the Cardinal was close to ending, we decided to leave in case there was a riot when both sides spilled into the street at the same time. "Let's head for the Intercontinental Hotel to watch the heads of state arrive for the luncheon," suggested Sean, who as a reporter had seen these events before.

We walked from the baseball stadium, across town, and up the hill to the Intercontinental Hotel to watch as Heads of State from all over the world and their wives were driven in Toyotas and dropped off at the door. Some were in suits, some in full African tribal outfits. "Who do you think that is?" I'd ask, amazed at the styles of the colorful dresses worn by the women.

Sean would reply something like, "Oh, that is the President of Oman," and give his name. This went on through multiple presidents and prime ministers. He knew most of them. When Daniel Ortega drove his own Jeep to the party, both Sally and I recognized him without Sean's help.

And then came the Emperor! We had seen police practicing the routine the night before, as we sat in the Salvadoran restaurant near the Intercontinental Hotel. Vice-President Quale had flown his black bulletproof limo to Managua, along with a contingent of Republican Senators and Congressmen.

As we watched fascinated the night before, six local policemen on motorcycles, riding two by two, practiced leading the car along the road up to the Intercontinental Hotel, followed by six more policemen on motorcycles, riding two by two behind the limo. American flags flapped from both the right and left front bumpers of the limo. It looked weird the night before. On the day of the inauguration, the stretch limo containing Secret Service officers, Vice-President Dan Quale, and his wife Marilyn looked completely out of place compared to the chauffeur-driven four-door Toyotas delivering presidents and heads of state to the inauguration luncheon!

After all the luncheon guests had entered the Intercontinental, the three of us decided to go across the street to a little outdoor restaurant called Los Antojitos. The waiter sat us at a table, but he wouldn't take our order or serve us.

Sean spotted Governor Bruce Babbitt (former Democratic Governor of Arizona) and his wife Harriet sitting, also unserved, at another table, so he went over and asked, "Can we join you?" We spent an interesting hour chatting, while continuing to not-be-served, and watched busloads of people driving by waving blue and white flags and celebrating Doña Violeta's victory.

We never did figure out how the waiters knew we were not Republicans, except of course I had two cameras hanging around my neck and the three of us looked a little scruffy in our jeans, t-shirts, and tennis shoes. But Governor Babbitt... He wore a light weight summer suit, white shirt, and pastel colored tie, and his wife was in a dress...

Once the inauguration was over and April turned to May, it was time for me to move out of the Casa San Juan and into Marta's house. The politics quieted down. However, there was a fuss when it was learned that Daniel Ortega and others in the Sandinista government had taken possession of houses, cars, and money belonging to the government. The press called it 'La Piñata.' Apparently, the night before the inauguration they took everything they could get their hands on before giving up power, leaving the new government without physical or financial resources. For a party that prided itself on being for and with the poor, La Piñata made the Sandinistas look as corrupt as every other political party in Nicaragua... a bad omen for the years to come.

When Lorraine Spencer from Adoption International, the adoption agency in Omaha, called me a few days after the inauguration, I told her, "Not only is Roberto here, but there are two other kids who also need adoptive homes; Erik, an 8-year-old boy with cerebral palsy, and Eliodora, a 3-month-old baby girl with a double cleft palate and lip. All three of them need adoptive families, and they won't get them here."

"Okay," she replied, "Suzanne and I will come down in June to see what we can do to complete these adoptions."

In the meantime, Zaidy and I entered all the immunization data into my computer, so we could see who needed what shots when, without having to sift one by one through all 85 children's files.

I also entered data about the children—when they came in, when they left, when they were adopted, and what if anything was medically wrong with them.

In 1990, disabled children were integrated with normally developing children at Rolando Carazo. Eduardo Carson, the special education teacher from Toronto, believed firmly in the Normalization Principle. According to Eduardo, "Developmentally disabled children do better if they are raised around normal peers."

Rolando Carazo housed normally developing full-term newborn infants, some of whom were placed for adoption with well-off Nicaraguan families who couldn't have children. The Center also housed older infants and toddlers, who had arrived as newborns but were not placed for adoption, older abandoned children whose families could not be found, and infants and children under age 12 with disabilities.

Since there were more available infants than rich families asking to adopt, healthy infants grew older in the Center waiting for a family that never came. The lawyer in charge of adoptions for Mi Familia ignored infants over one month of age, so she could offer adoptive families a more recently born infant.

Older infants thus became the victims of Mi Familia's 'last in/first out' placement policy. I suspect it was not a consciously decided policy. It just happened.

Thinking from the point of view of the parents rather than the children, the attorney in charge of adoption would offer the couple the youngest baby available.

Since there always was a baby younger than one month, if an infant reached one month without being adopted, he/she would never be offered to a family for adoption. "Adoptive parents want newborns," the adoption attorney said, as adorable healthy infants grew older facing institutional rather than family care.

This doesn't have to be, I fumed. She is causing a terrible situation for these left-behind babies, whether she realizes it or not. These babies will grow up without a family and have trouble forming families when they're adults, because family life is learned.

"Why doesn't she recruit more families?" I grumbled to Zaidy. "This is ridiculous. Any family would love these children! You know where these kids are going to end up? In one of the S.O.S. group homes!" I moaned as I stomped around the infirmary frustrated and angry. "They need to be in families."

My anger was brought on by watching a series of adoptive families come to pick up their under-one-month-old babies. I saw one adoptive couple when I was outside playing with some of the preschool children.

The soon-to-be mother was dressed impeccably in an expensive tailored suit and very high heels. She was mid-thirties in age, tall for a Nicaraguan, even without the heels, with light brown hair and European features. She could easily have been a Spaniard. As she walked by I could see that her makeup was perfect, despite the blazing hot sun that was causing the rest of us to drip with sweat.

Her husband, walking by her side and holding her arm, was a few inches shorter than his wife, older at perhaps 50 years of age, a little overweight with darker skin and very Nicaraguan features. He was dressed in an expensive American suit and tie, rather than in an embroidered one-color guayabera shirt, favored by most middle class Nicaraguan men for important occasions.

"Zaidy, look at those people coming for the baby," I called out when I returned to the infirmary. "They look like the richest of the rich. Is Mi Familia not approving professionals to adopt? Teachers, doctors, lawyers, professors… they're not rich, but they would be able to raise a child. Why doesn't the adoption attorney recruit more families for these normal infants? Surely there are families from the educated class out there who would want them. Why does she think adoptive parents have to be super-rich?" Zaidy just shook her head at my outburst and rolled her eyes.

Marching around the room, angry and frustrated, I thought, how can I get through to the adoption attorney that all babies do better if they grow up in families, not institutions or group homes? I can't even set up a meeting with her.

I looked at one darling year-old baby girl standing up and hanging over the bars of her crib, with glazed eyes and downturned mouth, looking more depressed each day, as she grew older without a family. I'll bet that damn attorney doesn't even think about these kids. She seems to think only about the wealthy couples that come looking for a baby, rather than about the kids we have here.

These healthy babies at Rolando Carazo don't have a chance at a future if she doesn't find a family for them. I can't find families for them in the U.S. because Nicaragua doesn't allow international adoption, except for disabled children.

# Chapter 9

# David

One day, shortly after the inauguration, I noticed a little boy playing among the 3-year-olds and assumed he was the child of one of the educadoras. He was dressed in blue shorts, a red t-shirt and red sneakers, and his long black hair was full of curls that hung down over his ears and nearly covered his forehead. Perhaps one of the staff brought him to work with her today, I hypothesized. The child's behavior was so different from the other children his age, that he stood out among the 3-year-olds. *He looks too normal to be living here*, I thought. *He must live in a family and just be visiting today.*

When Zaidy came out into the yard, I pointed him out and asked, "Who does that kid in the red t-shirt and red sneakers belong to?" He was busy digging scoops of sand and dropping it into a toy dump truck in the middle of the large sandbox. As we continued to watch, he seemed intent on what he was building and later exchanged his truck for another with a playmate, without grabbing the truck he wanted or making a fuss.

She looked at me quizzically. "That's David. He's one of the kids in the cottage over there."

"He lives here?" I asked with astonishment.

"Yes, he has been here for months. He was abandoned in the North and brought here by Mi Familia after they searched for his family and couldn't find anyone."

"Do you think he is one of the orphans of war?"
"I don't know. We don't know that much about him."
"Is he eligible for adoption?"
"I think so; there's a document of abandonment in his file."

"I hope he is eligible for adoption," I said, thinking how easy he would be to place for adoption, especially with my new American friend Jennifer and her Nicaraguan husband, Ricardo.

Jennifer Lansing and I had met at the Casa San Juan right after I arrived. She came to visit me in April during Holy Week when she heard there was a new American in town. She wanted to welcome me and find out what I was doing in Nicaragua.

Jennifer had a Master's Degree in English as a Second Language and taught in a private school in Managua, where all subjects were taught in English. Most children studying there were from wealthy families, but each employee, from the teachers to the cleaning crew, received a scholarship for one of their own children.

Jennifer looked a lot like my graduate students in Nebraska. She was 29, tall at about 5'9", and slim, with long light-brown hair and hazel eyes. She had been teaching English in Nicaragua for over five years and loved teaching the children in her ESL classes.

Jennifer had grown up in Iowa and looked and spoke like a Midwesterner, with the clear 'white bread' Midwestern accent preferred by radio and TV stations for their news announcers. She and her Nicaraguan husband, Antonio, had been married for five years, and they planned to remain in Nicaragua indefinitely. They had no children yet. "We have been thinking of adopting," Jennifer told me when we first met. She had heard I was working with abandoned children at Rolando Carazo, and she also heard that I had been involved in finding adoptive parents for special-needs children in Nebraska. "My husband Antonio and I are very nervous about having a baby," she confided. "In fact, we don't want a baby. It would be too hard with me working all day. We'd like to adopt an older child who is out of diapers."

I burst out laughing! "Oh Jennifer, you don't know what you are asking for. Diapers are the least of your troubles with an adopted child." Getting more serious, I told her. "bonding and attachment takes place most strongly in those first couple of years. Children who are abandoned or removed from families for abuse or neglect and become available for adoption at an older age, frequently have major behavioral problems. Most can adjust eventually, but their behavior is way harder to deal with than diapers."

"I just don't think I could deal with a baby in diapers," she explained apologetically.

"OK, let me keep my eyes open for an older child that might be available for adoption," I said.

After a couple of weeks of observing David more closely and reading everything in his file, I realized he might fit well into Jennifer and Antonio's family, despite them not having had any parenting experience. In May, I called Jennifer and suggested she come visit me at Rolando Carazo. "There is a very normal looking 3-year-old boy you might be interested in," I told her. "He doesn't seem to have the behavioral problems I often see in older abandoned children."

When Jennifer arrived at the Center to visit me, I reminded her that we should not let anyone know that she was looking to adopt one of the children. I explained the plan. "We'll walk around the Center, look at the buildings like I was taking you on a tour, and when we get to his cottage, you can observe David." A bit afraid that she might reach out to touch him or pick him up, I said, "Remember, Just look. Don't touch. We can't let David or anyone else know you might be interested in adopting him."

We walked in and out of several cottages, with me acting like an English-speaking tour guide for a visiting American. We looked at the paintings of the individual children on the walls of the cottages. We inspected the swing set and ended up playing with the 3-year-olds in the sand box behind their cottage, with her keeping an eye on "the one in the red and white striped shirt."

Jennifer was smitten. "Oh, he is so cute, I know Antonio will want to adopt him," she said when we got away from the children and into the safety of Zaidy's office in the Infirmary.

After a few more minutes of exclaiming how cute he was, Jennifer asked, "How do we go about doing this?"

I told her that she and her husband would have to talk to the attorney that was in control of adoption. "No one at Rolando Carazo has any power to place these children for adoption. It is all done by attorneys at the central office of Mi Familia."

After I left Nicaragua in July, Jennifer's husband, Antonio, went to Mi Familia and told them he and Jennifer wanted to adopt David.

The adoption attorney was appalled! "Oh no. I'm sure you want to adopt a baby," she insisted. But they persevered, and by October they could take David home. Even though Jennifer was a U.S. citizen, since she and her husband lived in Nicaragua and planned to raise David there, they were allowed to legally adopt him.

"We really had to fight hard to get him." Jennifer told me later. "The Mi Familia attorney was bound and determined that only babies should be adopted."

"You know," I pointed out, "that is not too different from the U.S. 40-50 years ago in the 1940s and 1950s. Children older than a few weeks, or at most a few months, were considered older children and 'unadoptable.' Even when I started as an advocate for adoption in the early 1960s, social workers labeled most of the kids in state custody 'unadoptable,' even though they were legally free for adoption. The social workers were so sure no one would want older children, they made no effort to find families for them.

There was nothing wrong with those children except they weren't newborns… babies that child advocates grew to sarcastically call 'infants with sterling silver stamped on their bottoms.'"

On a Sunday night in early May, while I was reading in my room, Lorraine Spencer called from Adoption International, the international adoption agency in Omaha, to say she might have families for Roberto and Erik and was working on a family for baby Eliadora. Oh wow, I thought. We may be able to get these disabled kids out of here and into families after all.

Because of the adoption law that forbade international adoption, I knew that only disabled children had a chance of being released by the Nicaraguan government for adoption, with the idea that only outside the country could they get the needed medical treatment. The normally developing infants, not adopted in their first month of life and growing up in cribs without a mother to take care of them, would not be freed by the government for international adoption. They would grow up in group homes or institutions in Nicaragua, not in families.

I need to think about how I can encourage the social workers at Rolando Carazo and the attorney at Mi Familia to look for more Nicaraguan adoptive families, I thought as I approached the bus stop at Siete-Sur the next morning. I understand that people who are so poor they cannot feed their families are not going to be interested in adopting another child, but surely there are professionals, (teachers, social workers, engineers, doctors, lawyers, etc.) that either don't have children or want to add to their families by adopting a child in need.

Why don't the social workers here go look for those families? I fretted, remembering my similar complaints and frustrations back in the 1960s when I was recruiting adoptive families as a volunteer in Nebraska for what were called "unadoptable" children. Why is this so hard? I wanted to scream as I pushed my way off the bus and started walking up the hill.

As I walked the two blocks up the inclined street from the bus stop to Rolando Carazo, I stopped worrying about Nicaraguan social workers not looking for adoptive families and started paying more attention to the weight of the laptop computer I carried every day in its black Land's End briefcase. This thing is too heavy, I complained to myself silently. The computer was indeed heavy, much heavier than laptops today. By lugging it every day up this hill, I was wearing out my arms, and no amount of changing it from arm to arm made it any lighter.

How do the women here carry those heavy baskets of vegetables and fruit all day? I wondered… On their heads, I realized, but how? I began to look at the fruit and vegetable sellers more closely. At every chance encounter, I snuck up close behind a woman balancing a heavy basket on her head to see how she did it, or watched a woman surreptitiously from a distance as she lifted the big basket off her head and set it down on the sidewalk. From what I could see, every woman had a dish towel rolled into a circular pad which she put on top of her head, before lifting the heavy basket onto it. The dish towel made her head flat and distributed the weight better, so she wasn't carrying the basket on just the ridge on top of her skull.

I can do that, I thought, and planned to practice dish towel wrapping and head-carrying of the computer around the house, until I got so good I wouldn't drop it. By the end of May, I had it down pat, and walked to and from the bus stop, looking a bit odd, balancing a heavy black briefcase on my head.

Over the weekend, I had managed to get my hands on a baby carrier, so whenever Eliadora was awake, I could strap her to me. Although the carrier was designed to keep the baby in front of me facing my chest, I figured out a way to put her in it so she was looking forward and could watch the world go by. We were a duo, all day, every day, walking tethered together all over the Infirmary and outside among the various cottages, like two peas in a pod. We looked at trees when the leaves finally came out after the rains started May 20th. We watched the traffic, sitting on the front steps of the center facing the busy highway going south. And when I needed to teach, she was right there like a kangaroo joey looking out of her pouch at my audience.

Since I planned to train the two social workers at the Rolando Carazo Center in adoption recruitment techniques, I hired a university educated Nicaraguan woman, Lastenia Suarez, to help me write a small training manual with adoption recruitment techniques explained in Spanish. I thought the social workers might recruit adoptive families more easily if they had a written how-to book.

The writing didn't go well! Lastenia was both confused by my poor Spanish and, more importantly, didn't agree with my premise.

She was incredulous that anyone would want to adopt any child other than a healthy newborn under one month old. Instead of helping me write the booklet in Spanish, when I asked her how to write a sentence so it was grammatically correct, Lastenia kept telling me "This will not work. No one wants to adopt these older children." Why am I paying this woman? I wondered.

Sitting across the desk from Lastenia in the social work office, frustrated with my lack of language skills and her refusal to translate correctly something she didn't agree with, I thought about my fights with social workers in the early 1960s in Nebraska. Shaking my head in frustration I thought, where have I heard this theme before? "Everyone wants a newborn. No one wants to adopt these kids… " but… IT IS NOT TRUE. Families come forward for them if they know about them. We understand that now in Nebraska. Why not here in Nicaragua?

Marielena understood my Spanish better when I argued with Lastenia about recruitment techniques, but she didn't agree with my ideas either. In addition, she pointed out, "Most people in Nicaragua don't have phones and couldn't call the agency even if they were interested." This was before the era of universal cell phones. Marielena's insight was good, because I had not thought about the presence or absence of telephones. But her refusal to even consider the idea of special needs adoption finally boiled down to a fundamental cultural belief which she explained to me, "Nicaraguans can't and won't adopt older or disabled children. Americans and Europeans are different, so they must do it for us."

Adoption of older or disabled children was not the only place I began to see the We are not able, so you must do it for us dependency attitude. I don't know if this is an attitude of long duration in Nicaragua or one caused by the thousands of volunteers and millions of dollars that poured into Nicaragua from European and American non-governmental organizations after the Triumph of the Sandinista Revolution in 1979. During the 80s, people in Nicaragua learned to act as if the only way to get anything was to beg for it from an NGO or from European or American visitors to Nicaragua. Dependency remains a major problem, especially for those Nicaraguans who came of age in the 1980s. It has taken years for younger Nicaraguans, born after 1990, to develop more of a 'can do' attitude.

Two of the children in the infirmary had hydrocephalus. Ana Maria was four-years-old with an enormous head, even bigger than a fully inflated basketball. Her head, full of spinal fluid, weighed probably 10-15 pounds like a giant watermelon, so she couldn't move it. She had a tiny dark brown body that she also couldn't move unaided. The crib she was in was only 36" long, made for a newborn, so her head, which filled nearly half of the crib, touched the top and her feet the bottom of the crib. Fortunately, she could stretch completely out, but only barely.

Her black hair was thin and completely worn off in back where she lay for hours, face up, on the white sheet-covered mattress.

Ana Maria had broken skin, like a bed sore, on the back of her head, which Zaidy treated several times a day to prevent more infection. Surprisingly, her sores did not smell. In fact, the only smell in the room was the antiseptic which the limpiadoras mopped on the floor two or three times a day to keep the room clean.

Ana Maria's eyes were brown, and bulged out because of the pressure of the fluid in her brain behind them. She could look down to see her feet, which made the whites of her eyes visible at the top, something doctors call 'sunset eyes,' a sure signal of intracranial pressure. I was afraid to pick her up, for fear of hurting her, although I was not put off by her disabilities. I was so used to children with disabilities, from my high school experiences at Easter Seal Camp and my continuing interest in special-needs children as I got older, that I could look in her eyes and see the person within, without being distracted by the unnatural look of some of her body parts. We connected when I told her, "Mi nombre es Ana, tambien (My name is Ann too)."

Ana Maria couldn't talk, but she could hear and loved music. Eduardo and I hung a bright red tape player on the end of her bed which she could see, and we turned on the music when she was awake. She could move only her eyes, but it was evident that she understood a lot, and recognized us with a smile when we talked to her. She did not appear to be in much pain, despite being trapped in a body she could not move. I think she understood my Spanish, and the expressions in her eyes showed she was with us. "The lights are on, and someone is home," I remarked to Eduardo in English.

Ana Maria knew what was going on around her, which made Eduardo and me almost apoplectic when Mi Familia bought a small wooden casket for her and put it in the corner of her room standing it up on its end.

"We all know she is going to die soon... but a casket? Where she can see it? Don't they know that she can think and understand?" I complained bitterly to Marielena, the Director of the center, but she told me the order from the central office of Mi Familia was to "put it in her room," so she had to leave it there. Unbelievable bureaucratic insensitivity made worse by unbelievable fear of the central office.

The little boy, Bryan, was a larger problem for me. A pretty baby, although his head was also much too big for his scraggly body, Bryan had light skin and blond/brown hair. His eyes were a hazel blue. I often wondered if the lack of color in his skin and hair was due to anemia, or whether it was natural. Bryan was only 13-months-old and cried constantly with pain. We had no painkillers to give him, and nothing seemed to comfort him. He cried when he was held. He cried when he was put down. I think his head must have ached all the time, like someone with a severe migraine. It was driving me crazy that we couldn't do anything to stop his suffering. I felt like I wanted to pick him up, but when I did, it didn't make him feel any better, and it made me feel utterly useless. After a while I left him to the care of his educadora, as I couldn't stand listening to his crying in pain. I wondered if Bryan ever slept. All day long when I was in the Center he cried or he screamed.

The educadoras who cared for him were saints. They never got angry or yelled at him. They never ignored him and left him in the bed crying. They always picked him up and held him and tried to comfort him. But nothing worked. While Eduardo and I could entertain Ana Maria with music and talking to her, nothing worked with Bryan.

I asked Zaidy, "What do you think will help them? They both are uncomfortable, and Bryan is miserable. Surely there is something we can do to make them more comfortable."

Zaidy mentioned that getting the pressure off the back of her head would certainly help Ana Maria's bed sores on her scalp. "Maybe getting Bryan in a weight free suspension will help," she hypothesized when I suggested water bed mattresses for the two of them. The next time Lorraine called, I asked her to bring two crib-size waterbed mattresses, when she and Suzanne came down.

"Maybe that will relieve some of the pressure from Ana Maria and Bryan's super-large heads," I told Lorraine when she called. "We have to do something."

I cautioned her, "You need to find water bed mattresses to fit a crib. For God's sake, don't bring full-size mattresses, since we don't have enough space for anything bigger than what will fit in their cribs."

A few days later, Lorraine called and told me, "We got the mattresses! They are boxed up and ready to go. The man at the store gave them to us at a sale price when he heard what they were going to be used for."

I was ecstatic. "Maybe those kids will get some relief for once in their short lives," I said to Zaidy. "The mattresses were a bit expensive, but if they work, it will be worth it. I can't listen to Bryan cry much more!"

Lorraine called the next week to say that a doctor in Omaha was interested in adopting Eliadora. "Can you measure the baby's head and see if other head measurements have been taken previously?" Lorraine asked.

"Are you serious?" I replied. I had never heard of measuring a baby's head. The next day, I approached Zaidy and sheepishly asked her, "Do you know how to measure a baby's head?" After asking it, I realized it was a stupid question. Of course, she did. She was an RN. Realizing from her response that she had done this many times, I asked, "did anyone measure Eliadora's head previously?" We looked through the files and found an earlier measurement. When Lorraine called back, I gave her the head measurements at two different ages, and she forwarded the information to Dr. Mary Kay Bowen. Apparently, the measurements indicated normal head growth, so Mary Kay started getting documents together to come to Nicaragua to adopt the baby.

I decided I wanted to buy something for Eliadora. I heard there was a Dollar Store in Managua near Metro Centro where you could buy things not available elsewhere... if you had dollars. I didn't know what to expect when I approached the one-story-tall building that reminded me of a large supermarket. The man at the door demanded that I show him the dollars I had before he would let me in.

The building reminded me of a Post Exchange, except this was not on a U.S. military base. It was a large plain building, situated in an empty field, in an area of Managua the Nicaraguan government had wishfully called Metro Centro. The old center of town had been reduced to rubble in the 1972 earthquake, 18 years before. The government apparently planned to build a new city center at Metro Centro. But in the meantime, the Dollar Store was the only building located there, in a big empty field.

Inside the warehouse-like store there was very little light. The walls were dark green which made the inside of the store even darker, like a cave. There was no organization of materials. Things for sale were placed here and there among cardboard boxes, resembling a buy-in-bulk grocery store. Stepping over and around small merchandise, I continued to search unsuccessfully for the baby department.

If I can just find the baby department, surely they will have a mobile that I can hang over her crib, I told myself, as I struggled to orient myself in the darkness. Every baby department has mobiles. After searching around the entire store and finding only car batteries and a few pieces of furniture, I had to admit that maybe The Dollar Store didn't have a baby department or any mobiles for babies. What else can I get her? I thought as I looked around. Suddenly, I spotted a stuffed Minnie Mouse doll that Eliadora could grasp with her hands But, that was about the extent of the toy choices. Even in the supposedly most-stocked store in Managua, there were no other baby toys.

I still wanted her to have a mobile. I remembered when my son PJ was a few months old, he punched and kicked at the birds that hung over his crib, yelling at them, and having a great time as the birds flew around randomly with each kick. If I can't find a mobile, I'll make one, I decided. In the Dollar Store, there were bows for sale to stick on gift packages. I bought a bunch of them in yellow, red, green, and blue to create bright spheres by sticking two bows of the same color to each other. I had done this years previously when I had four preschool children, a dog, a cat, and a Christmas tree. When the tree would inevitably crash down, I wanted only colorful spheres of ribbon, not breakable ornaments to go flying. Remembering those colorful, but safe, Christmas decorations, I made a string of multicolored spheres and strung them across Eliadora's crib for visual stimulation. With satisfaction, I thought, Well, this isn't as good as birds to kick, but it's better than looking at that bare ceiling.

One day toward the middle of May when I arrived for work at Rolando Carazo, Eliadora looked sick. Generally, as soon as I arrived, I fed her using a bottle with a baby nipple that was cut open. She could not suck, since she had no palate in the roof of her mouth. To feed her I had to hold her up into a sitting position, drip milk into her mouth a little at a time, and let her swallow it.

When I got to the Center that morning, it appeared someone else had already fed her. Eliadora was breathing very fast, so Zaidy listened to her chest. "I can hear noises in her lungs," Zaidy said. "She may have inhaled her milk." With that information, Zaidy and Marielena decided that Eliadora should go to the hospital.

A young auxiliadora (nurse's aide) from Rolando Carazo, Lily Caldera, and I went with Eliadora in one of the Center's trucks down the street about a half mile to the Hospital Velez Paiz, the national children's hospital. When we got to the hospital I was overwhelmed with the crowd of people waiting there. In every corridor, along every wall, mothers with babies on their laps sat waiting in metal chairs for a doctor to diagnose and treat their infant. There may have been older children at the hospital, but all those I saw in the halls were lactantes (babies still nursing). Mothers, some looking like teenagers of 15 or 16, sat quietly nursing their babies in every chair, in every corridor of the hospital, patiently waiting… and waiting… and waiting.

A tall dark-haired young man in a white lab coat approached. His name, Dr. Edgardo Mesa, was written on the ID tag attached to his white coat. He was a pediatric resident, looked about 23 years old, and like most Nicaraguans was very friendly. He introduced himself as Dr. Mesa, asked a few questions, and then listened to Eliadora's lungs. As soon as he heard the rattling, he took us to have x-rays. Dr. Mesa told Lily to hold the baby up in front of her chest while they took the x-ray. I was horrified, since they didn't even ask Lily if she was pregnant. Lily sat upright on the x-ray table and held the baby in front of the film and the film in front of her own belly and chest. The x-ray technician aimed the X-ray at them and clicked. I stood at the side of the table in shocked silence, remembering with horror my impression of medical care in Nicaragua in 1984. It hadn't improved.

We waited a half hour until the doctor showed us the film. There were hundreds of white specs on the x-ray. She had indeed inhaled her milk. "Look," Dr. Mesa said, pointing to the specks all over her lungs. "She has inhalation pneumonia. I will admit her to the hospital." As he thumbed through her medical chart, which Zaidy had sent along with us, Dr. Mesa noticed that Eliadora hadn't had a BCG shot and wanted to give her one. I protested, "This baby is going to the US for adoption. They don't give the BCG there, so they can use the skin test if she is exposed to TB."

Dr. Mesa warned me, "There might be children in the room with her upstairs that have active TB," a sure sign the hospital didn't isolate infectious patients. But, despite his concern, I found later that the doctor hadn't ordered a BCG shot for her. I made a mental note to tell her adoptive mother to get her a skin test for TB as soon as they got to the US.

When we got upstairs to the second floor, I peeked into two large rooms and could see metal cribs with chipped paint, and a mother sitting quietly next to the crib of each infant or child. The room where Eliadora would be kept, located at the very end of the hall, was large and airy, with a high ceiling and high windows that reached from waist level to the ceiling.

Her room had seven cribs and a large laundry-style sink located at the end of the room between two windows that looked down at the Pepsi stand in front of the hospital. Eliadora's bed was just inside the door, beside another set of windows which looked out at the parking lot at the side of the hospital.

There were lightweight beige colored cotton drapes on all the windows, which blew around flapping like sails when there was a storm outside. The tall windows were made of glass slats that could rotate open or shut. The walls were ugly hospital green, while the floor was covered with reddish-brown floor tiles. Just outside the room was a small enclave with a desk for the nurse who was in charge. It was here that the nurse kept medical records and where she organized the baby bottles before she delivered them to each crib. Mothers were expected to feed their babies. When the mother was not there, the bottle of milk remained unused in the corner of the baby's crib, while he howled with hunger. Generally, one of the other mothers, not the nurse, would take the milk and feed him until his mother returned.

One day, one of the mothers left and didn't come back. After about four hours we finally realized that the baby was being abandoned in the typical Nicaraguan way: take him to a hospital and give a non-existent address. If after 24 hours a mother or other family member did not return to care for the baby, his case would be turned over to a Mi Familia social worker who searched for the mother. In the meantime, those of us on the ward took turns feeding and changing "our" abandoned baby. If Mi Familia did not find the mother, Rolando Carazo would soon be receiving this baby when he was released from the hospital. "It looks like we are going to get you, bebe," I told him as I fed and changed him. "I hope you have a name and a birthdate, so we don't have to guess your age and name you Jose (or maybe Estevan) Carazo."

The common practice at Rolando Carazo was to give all children who were brought to the Center without identification the last name of Carazo and a regular first name. Zaidy then guessed the age of the baby and counted back to the month he/she was most likely born. The first of that month was then chosen as the birthdate. As I began entering information about the 80+ children at the Center into my little computer, I had noticed that many children had Carazo as a last name. It was when I asked Zaidy why so many of the children were Carazos, that she told me about their policy for naming foundlings and for deciding on birthdates. For older children, she would check their teeth. Seriously malnourished children might be very small and look much younger than they are, but despite malnutrition, teeth tend to erupt at the expected age.

All the babies with upper respiratory infections were kept in the room with Eliadora. I assumed the other room housed children with diarrhea, as those were the two diagnoses that were typically made in Nicaragua: URI or Diarrhea.

As I looked around the room when we first entered, I noticed that all the babies and toddlers had splints taped around one hand with a needle permanently imbedded in a vein in that hand. What is going on? I wondered. Is this a case of everybody getting the same treatment? I was not reassured when I found out later, no matter their diagnosis, all children were getting IV penicillin.

The nurse came to insert a needle into Eliadora's hand. First, she tried the right hand. Eliadora screamed immediately when she felt the needle. I noticed that the nurse was moving the needle around as if she were still looking for a vein. The baby continued to scream as I held her tight in my lap. In frustration, the nurse withdrew the needle from her hand, causing a stream of blood to drip onto the tile floor. Maybe that's why the floors are reddish, to cover the bloodletting, I thought. Then she took the Eliadora's left hand and aimed the needle where she thought a vein should be. More screaming, but still no success. In desperation, the nurse shifted her focus to the wrists, first the right wrist, then the left, bending them almost to the breaking point. By this time the Eliadora was screaming hysterically, thoroughly traumatized, while I grew more anxious with every failed stick. You're treating her like a pin cushion, I thought to myself in English.

The nurse, whom I decided was totally incompetent, decided to try to hit a vein in the left ankle and then the right. Eleven times she had tried to hit a vein and failed. It was obvious that this nurse didn't know how to start an IV. When she said she was going to try to hit the vein in Eliadora's head, I said "No Más! Basta!" (No More! Enough!) The thought that she might cause an infection in the baby's head, or even in her brain, seemed very likely to me, since the nurse clearly didn't know what she was doing, and infection control in the hospital seemed missing entirely.

Gathering up all my knowledge of hospitals and taking control of the rapidly deteriorating situation, I announced to the nurse, "If the baby needs penicillin, she can have it orally. She doesn't need an IV." The nurse looked angrily at me, as if she wanted to grab the baby out of my arms. But she turned on her heels and marched out of the room, leaving me to wonder what type of trouble I had gotten myself into with the hospital.

An hour later, a very angry woman doctor stormed in and shouted, "Are you a doctor? How do you know she doesn't need an IV?"

I replied, "The nurses here are incompetent, and they will infect her brain if they try to put it in her head. In the US, doctors give penicillin orally. We don't even know if the baby has a bacterial infection. All we know is that she has milk in her lungs. Give her oral penicillin if you think she needs penicillin, but no more needles."

The doctor, who was likely a medical student or a resident, stormed out muttering words under her breath to look for some oral penicillin. Round one to Grandma!

The auxiliadora, Lily Caldera, went back to Rolando Carazo in the truck, and sent over Doña Lidia, the older woman who had fed Eliadora from a spoon when she first came to the Center in March suffering from third stage malnutrition. Eliadora had spent six weeks in the hospital in Leon after she was born. There, no one knew how to feed a baby with a cleft palate, and they had no feeding tubes. Six weeks of poor nursing care had resulted in a seriously malnourished and dehydrated baby.

The Leon hospital transferred her to Velez Paiz Children's Hospital in Managua where Dr. Reynaldo Blandon, a second-year pediatric resident, did a cut down of a vein in her groin to give her suero (an IV form of pedialite) for the dehydration.

When she was stabilized, they sent her to Rolando Carazo and Doña Lidia began slowly feeding her milk from a spoon. I doubt if they gave her formula, because at that time baby formula cost about $7 a can and was pretty much available only at the Dollar Store. For the infants at Rolando Carazo, the cooks diluted cow's milk with water to make it more digestible, and added sugar for taste and for calories. I suspect Eliadora got the watered-down version as well. However, little by little, after receiving tiny teaspoons of watered-down milk hour after hour from Doña Lidia, the baby started to gain weight.

She was back to about 6 pounds the day I arrived on the scene in April when she was 11 weeks old. She began to be fed from a bottle with a large hole in the nipple. But now, just a few weeks later, she was back in the hospital again, with inhalation pneumonia. Does no one in this whole country know how to take care of a baby with a cleft? I thought.

When Doña Lidia came for the night shift, I left the hospital and went across Managua in a cab to the one place where I could send and receive a fax. I sent a fax to Suzanne and Lorraine at Adoption International in Omaha, "Have the doctor call me. The baby is in the hospital and needs better medical care. I think she should come down now and not wait until June."

Mary Kay, the baby's soon to be adoptive mother, called me by phone and asked if the baby was being fed with a tube. "No, we are feeding her from a bottle with a large hole in the nipple, holding her upright and trying to keep it out of her lungs. They don't have feeding tubes here." I told her, and paused to let that sink in. "You need to come now," I begged. "The baby's not doing well… and bring feeding tubes."

"I'll come as soon as I can get a ticket and get medicines and feeding tubes," Mary Kay promised.

"By the way, what are you calling her?" I asked.

"Katie," she replied.

When I returned to the hospital in the morning to relieve Doña Lidia and resume my all-day shift, Eliadora, who would soon be named Katie, was still breathing very fast. I spotted an oxygen tank and commandeered it. When I held the tube under her nose, her color improved dramatically and her respiration slowed. Clearly she needed oxygen.

Soon a nurse came by and told me, "Stop wasting the oxygen. That is all we have for the entire ward." I stopped, but Katie became blue again. So, every 30 minutes I gave her oxygen, until another nurse finally took the entire oxygen container into a different room.

I was furious with the nurses. What is wrong with them?! I thought. They don't know what they are doing, and Katie could pay with her life for their ignorance! I was frantic with fear for her.

Later I learned from a Nicaraguan doctor that nurses in Nicaragua had very little training. The doctors didn't trust them to take pulse, respiration, temperature, or blood pressure readings, let alone anything more advanced. The auxiliadoras (nurses' aides) had only primary school education (3rd to 6th grade). The nurses had a high school diploma and practical training in a technical college, like a licensed practical nurse in the U.S. UNAN-Managua did have 5-year professional nurses training leading to a degree, but most nurses in the public hospitals were little more than nurses' aides. I knew in an emergency the nurses would not be knowledgeable or skilled. "Katie, you and I are on our own." I warned the baby, as I went on the hunt for another oxygen tank.

The medical students floating in and out of the room were teenagers or in their early 20s. Students in Nicaragua enter medical school straight from high school at age 17. The residents weren't much older, at 22 or 23, and were there only occasionally. In the ten days we were in Velez Paiz Hospital, I never saw a full-fledged attending physician. The residents were practicing medicine on their own, with very little supervision. I have no idea if the residents even consulted with their attending about their cases. The attending physicians clearly did not lay eyes on the patients their residents were managing.

I had a baby in need of oxygen and a feeding tube, whose heart might give out at any moment from the stress of breathing so fast, in a hospital that lacked feeding tubes and was low on oxygen, with unskilled nurses and a medical staff younger than my undergraduate students back home.

Katie and I were in deep trouble, but the baby in the next bed was worse. She was unconscious! As I fussed and fumed about how to get oxygen, a mother from the other room came in to announce that twins had arrived dehydrated from diarrhea, and one had just died in the next room. Most of the mothers from our room went to look and to sympathize with the grieving mother next door, each one thinking I am sure, "My baby could be next."

It is a myth that parents in developing countries don't value life, and when a baby dies they don't care as much as we do. They care a lot! It is a very big deal! Often the mother must deal with the baby's death by herself, if she is far from home. Perhaps she must take the dead baby wrapped in a little blanket on a public bus back to her pueblo for burial. In public, parents appear to cope well with death, perhaps better than we would. But that doesn't mean they don't care. They care as much, if not more, than we do.

Children are cherished in Nicaragua. They are the riches of a family and much loved. Walk around a barrio with a camera, and mothers and grandmothers will pop out of shacks with a baby for you to admire and photograph. When they see you coming, they sometimes duck back into the house to get a pink bonnet so the baby will look even cuter. They cherish their little ones.

In the hospital that day, Mariela Juarez, the mother standing alongside the nearby crib which held her unconscious baby, and I were in the same boat... totally desperate. We both knew our babies were in serious trouble.

Mariela, an evangelical, began praying and singing hymns and making incantations over her unconscious baby girl, asking for a miracle from her God. It suddenly occurred to me that I was doing the same thing by trying to engage the gods of modern medicine in the US to help Katie. We both were helpless to save them by ourselves, and we knew it. We waited together for our respective gods to intervene. I never felt closer to another person before or after. Despite our differences in education and class, we were the same. Helpless, we waited, together, like soldiers in a fox hole, not knowing what was going to happen, but fearing the worst.

The gods smiled favorably on both of us. Her baby became conscious the next day, and I received a phone call from Suzanne when I got home that night that Mary Kay was ready to travel with feeding tubes and medicine. She would be arriving the next evening on the flight from Houston.

## Chapter 10

## International Adoption

On the day Dr. Mary Kay Bowen was to arrive with medicines and feeding tubes, Gail Wilson, the American reporter I had met in April at the Casa San Juan, picked me up in her red sports car at the Velez Paiz Hospital at 6:00 p.m. We would go from the hospital to the airport to get Mary Kay, driving along the Caretera Norte, from the west side of the city where the hospital was located, clear across the entire city of Managua to the most northeast corner of the capitol, where the Augusto Sandino Airport was located. Although it was an International Airport, the Managua airport in 1990 was smaller than the Grand Island airport in rural Nebraska. There were no gates. Arriving passengers walked down rollaway portable steps pushed up to the door of the plane, walked across the tarmac, and entered the one-story-tall brown airport building to go to Immigration and then take their luggage through Customs.

"I have no idea what she looks like," I told Gail. Observing the parade of arriving passengers, many of them Americans, I whispered, "I hope we are able to recognize her," as I scanned the faces of people exiting into the airport waiting room, one by one from Customs.

Eventually, I spotted a very tall, very heavy, and very white woman anxiously scanning the waiting crowd, continually turning her head, which was covered in sweaty dark hair, obviously searching for someone. Maybe that's her, I thought as I waved.

Looking relieved, she waved back and mouthed, "Ann?"

I nodded and smiled. "Welcome the Nicaragua," I said when she reached us. "You have no idea how happy I am to see you."

"Can we go to the hospital now?" Mary Kay asked unexpectedly, even though it was 9:00 p.m. and dark.

"We may have trouble getting in since Doña Lidia is already there." I cautioned her. "I have a pass, and Jose, the night guard, is used to seeing me. But getting the three of us in… " My voice trailed off as I thought of the upcoming confrontation with Jose when we reached the entrance to the hospital.

When we arrived at Velez Paiz Hospital, I announced to Jose, as authoritatively as I could in my bad Spanish, "The specialist doctor from the United States needs to see the baby NOW." As I spoke, I curled my thumb and forefinger into a circle leaving my other three fingers straight and brought my arm down strongly, as I said "ya" (now). In Nicaragua, gesturing with a hand in that position means that the speaker is serious. Mothers use it all the time when they are determined to make a point to a recalcitrant child. Jose hesitated for a second, started to argue with me by saying "only one," hesitated again, and finally let the three of us in.

When we got upstairs, Doña Lidia was standing beside the crib. The other mothers in the room knew that the adoptive mother was coming soon, so they gathered around to see the first meeting of mother and child. Mary Kay's first response was "Oh, she's so small!" Since I had seen her every day, Katie looked normal to me. However, at 4 months, she weighed only 7 pounds, the size of a newborn. Mary Kay held her for a few minutes, snuggling the tiny baby into her voluptuous breasts, kissing her on the top of her head and murmuring her name and mother words to her in English. All the other mothers sighed and smiled seeing the joy in the new mother's face and understanding that the little orphan baby they had gotten to know, now had a mother to care for her. Since there was nothing we could do at that hour, we left Katie with Doña Lidia for the night, and Gail drove us to Marta Mejia's house in Centro America where I had been living since early May.

That morning, when Mary Kay left Omaha to fly to Managua, the temperature had been 71 degrees. In Managua, when she arrived it registered 96, even though it was after dark. The rains that would drop the temperature somewhat had not yet started. Mary Kay sweated profusely with the heat, because of the 25-degree change in temperature, and because of her size. By the time we reached Marta's, the heat and the new role of being a first-time mother had overwhelmed her, bringing her to tears.

If she could not adjust to the heat, it looked like I might have a problem on my hands. There was no air-conditioning in Marta's house.

There was no air-conditioning in the hospital. The busses and the taxis we needed to take were full of hot sweaty people sharing the ride. Even Gail's sports car was hot. The only place I knew that had air-conditioning was the little hotel and restaurant next to the Casa San Juan where I had eaten dinner most nights, before I moved to Marta's.

The next morning, Mary Kay and I took a taxi to the hospital, so Mary Kay could demonstrate to the pediatric residents how to insert a feeding tube, using Katie as a model. As we approached the room filled with expectant young doctors, Mary Kay said to me quietly in English, "I don't do this at home. The nurses do."

"Well, fake it!" I hissed, a bit startled. "They think you are the big specialist from the US… and for God's sake don't say you work on the transplant team. Nicaraguans believe that Americans adopt babies to transplant their organs into sick American or Israeli children."

Mary Kay looked at me quizzically. "I'm serious," I said. "There are stories in the Latin American papers from time to time about bodies of children being found with their livers or kidneys missing. The 'find' is always in another country and never documented, and the story is typically about a Jewish kid in Israel who needs a liver or a kidney or a heart."

"You've got to be kidding!" she replied.

"No. It is an urban myth, but many people, even educated ones, believe it although it is patently false. There is a flavor of anti-Semitism in these stories as well. So, not a word about being on the Nebraska Medical Center's transplant team... and speak slowly so I can translate."

Carrying Katie, we walked into the room filled with about 15 of the hospital's pediatric residents. I introduced Dr. Bowen to the expectant group of young doctors, and she began to demonstrate how to insert a feeding tube into a baby's stomach.

First, she placed the tube on top of the baby and measured the distance from Katie's mouth to the point on her belly where she knew the stomach was located. She made a mark on the tube that showed how far down the tube should go to reach the baby's stomach. Then she picked Katie up, holding her one-handed on her left arm and hand, something she had obviously done before with many babies, and with her right hand, she popped the tube down Katie's throat. It went down slick as a whistle with no complaint from the baby. I was impressed.

The residents seem to understand how to do it, I thought. Although they look like they have never seen a tube being placed into a baby's stomach... or even seen a feeding tube before.

After she popped the tube down, Mary Kay asked for a glass of water to make sure air was not coming out of the other end of the tube. That would happen if the tube were in the baby's lungs and not in her stomach. "No bubbles," she said to the residents, pointing to the end of the feeding tube in the glass of water and showing them how to look for bubbles. When Mary Kay was sure the feeding tube was in the baby's stomach and not her lungs, she taped the tube to the side of the Katie's face with 2" wide white tape.

After asking for a bottle of warmed formula, she filled a large syringe from it and demonstrated to the residents how to inject food by placing the big formula-filled syringe into the end of the tube and slowly pushing the liquid into Katie's stomach. With no more milk going into them, Katie's lungs began to clear. In a few days, she was breathing easier. It was time to make plans to take the baby home.

When we went to Rolando Carazo to arrange with Marielena for her to come home with us, we found that while I was in the hospital with Katie, the government had replaced Marielena with a new director who was not a member of the Sandinista Party. The new government had begun to replace all employees of government agencies, based on their political party.

After we asked her to let the baby come home with us to Marta's house, Edipsia Balladares, the new director of the Rolando Carazo Center stated, "When Eliadora is released from the hospital, she needs to return here to the Rolando Carazo Center."

Earlier at the hospital, Mary Kay had confided to me, "I have medicines to give her once we get her out of here."

I told the new Director of Rolando Carazo, "The doctora has medicines that the baby needs, so she needs to stay with her."

The discussion went around and around for a while, with Senora Balladares saying several times, "She can't go with the doctora, the adoption isn't authorized yet."

I countered by repeating, "The doctora brought medicines to treat her. She has to stay with her."

I could see we were getting nowhere. So, I made a counter proposal. "We will move into the Centro Rolando Carazo, and la doctora and I will sleep on two of the bottom bunks of the little wooden beds in the baby and toddler room."

Sra. Balladares, startled, thought it over for a second, apparently realizing that even I was too big for a bottom bunk, and came up with another suggestion. "Eliadora can go with Anita to her casa sustituta (foster home)"

I laughed to myself, I suppose the vision of a 6' tall, 300 pound, lily white American woman sleeping in one of the bottom bunks in a cottage filled with toddlers was more than she could comfortably deal with.

With me as the 'casa sustituta' (substitute home), we began the process of leaving the hospital. Katie's temperature was normal. Her breathing was normal. All she needed was another x-ray to show that her lungs were clear.

For the entire ten days, Dr. Karla Fuentes, a first-year pediatric resident at Velez Paiz, was her assigned doctor and helped us through the process. Karla was an attractive 26-year-old woman, who stood about 5'3" tall, with brown skin and curly black hair that hung down loosely over her shoulders.

She had graduated from the College of Medicine at UNAN in Leon, and spent two years doing her 'social services' in Managua with researchers from Tufts University, before she was selected for a pediatric residency at the Velez Paiz Hospital, along with three of her fellow medical school classmates. She was anxious to spend time with us, since she attended English classes in the evenings at the UCA, and we were native speakers. She told us to call her Karla.

Karla sent us down to x-ray to get the 'all clear' film taken. Standing in line, Mary Kay, an observant pediatrician, noticed that the child to the left of us had a rash. I did not notice a thing, except that the room was hot and crowded. Mary Kay leaned down and whispered to me, "Oh my God, that child has measles," and in a single motion took Katie away from him by rotating to the right and walking to the farthest corner of the room with Katie in her arms.

I rather nonchalantly asked the mother in Spanish, "Does your baby have measles?"

"Si," the mother replied.

I stood in the line of parents and babies to hold our place while Mary Kay sheltered Katie in the corner of the room by the windows. After an hour, the x-ray was taken and showed Katie's lungs were clear of milk. Immediately we went upstairs looking for Karla.

"Katie was exposed to measles down in x-ray," I explained when we finally found Karla in the large room on the second floor which contained diarrhea patients. "Can you find some measles vaccine?" I asked.

Karla looked in the ward where Katie was living with the other children with upper respiratory infections, but there was no vaccine. She looked where the hospital kept supplies, but there was no vaccine there either. She looked all over the second floor, and still, no vaccine. She went to the emergency room. No vaccine. She went upstairs to the clinics. No vaccine. She went downstairs to x-ray. No vaccine. From top to bottom, in Velez Paiz Hospital, the national pediatric hospital of reference, Karla couldn't find one dose of measles vaccine!

I was stunned, and at a loss, but Karla called the local health clinic down the street. "Do you have measles vaccine?" she asked the nurse who answered.

"Yes," was the reply.

"We will be right there," Karla told her.

The three of us walked out of the hospital and marched half a mile down the sidewalk toward the neighborhood health clinic. Karla was dressed in jeans and a t-shirt, covered by her white physician's lab coat. Mary Kay tall and big, was dressed in dark slacks and a white flowing blouse, carrying tiny dark-skinned baby Katie dressed only in a diaper and wrapped in a white cotton blanket. I tagged along as a translator in my usual black slacks and a colorful peasant shirt. We were quite a sight marching down the Pan American Highway in the heat and humidity, with trucks, busses, and cars zipping by. After ten minutes, we finally got to the health center, with all of us, including the baby, dripping with sweat.

"We've come for the measles vaccination," Karla told the clinic nurse in Spanish as she greeted us at the door. "I'm the doctor that called you from Velez Paiz fifteen minutes ago."

"Oh, I'm sorry, we don't have any measles vaccine," the nurse reported. "But we do have some DPT vaccine. Would you like a DPT shot instead?" I just looked at her dumbfounded.

After realizing the nurse was serious, I whispered to Mary Kay, "Oh for God's sake!" and then translated the offer. Mary Kay, already red-faced and winded from the sun and the walk, looked ready to explode with anger and frustration.

"Gracias, no," Karla answered the nurse. "What we need is a measles immunization. The baby has been exposed to measles, not the other infections."

The nurse didn't seem to understand why we wouldn't accept a DPT shot instead of the measles shot, and looked a little hurt that we didn't agree to her substitution. I made a face at Karla as if to say, what is wrong with her?

Karla just smiled, but later explained, "The nurses here are not very well educated. We don't trust them with our patients."

Mary Kay was too hot and too tired from the walk to say much, but there wasn't any place for her to rest. We had to turn around and walk all the way back up the Pan American Highway to the hospital to formulate another plan.

After walking up the highway for 10 more minutes, we reached the hospital and slowly climbed the stairs to the second floor where I collapsed into a metal and wooden chair beside an empty crib in the URI room, thinking *Now what are we going to do?* Mary Kay, gasping for breath and sweating profusely, put Katie in her crib and sat down hard in the nearest chair. I was relieved to see Katie lying in the crib, as I was afraid Mary Kay might pass out while we were walking, but she wouldn't let either one of us carry the baby.

Karla went to look again throughout the hospital for measles vaccine. Finally, when searching through a cooler in one of the wards, she found some measles vaccine, but there were no syringes with it.

Karla came back to tell us she had found the vaccine. "It was in a cooler upstairs," she reported, "But there were no syringes or needles with it, so I have to search more places for those." She came back again in about 20 minutes to inform us, "I found a syringe, but no needle." The lack of a needle required another top to bottom search of the nation's most advanced children's hospital. Finally, Karla managed to find a needle, and Katie received her measles shot.

Since she had received a measles's immunization, the hospital insisted that she stay overnight for observation. By morning Katie was running a fever, so we had to spend yet another day and night at Velez Paiz. It had been 10 days for me… without lunch, and with only water to drink during the day from the big sink located between the windows in Katie's ward.

At 6:00 PM every afternoon, when I walked out of the hospital, I would buy a Pepsi-light from the stand and read the headlines of the papers that were lying there on the shelf. I became more concerned about the increasing conflicts between the new government and the workers. Trouble is coming, I surmised.

That night of the measles shot, after leaving Katie with Doña Lidia in the hospital, Mary Kay and I hailed a taxi to take us back to Marta's. After I gave the taxi driver the address, which began, 'del ceibo,' I asked him what the word ceibo meant.

"It's a big tree," he said.

"Is it a real tree, here in Managua?" I asked.

"Yes. It is here in Centro America," he replied. "I'll show it to you." He drove us past an enormous tree that I had never noticed before and pointed to it. "That's a ceibo," he said.

"Are there other ceibo trees in Managua?" I asked wondering why that large, but rather non-descript, tree was so important.

"Oh yes," he said looking at me as if should know. "There are lots of them."

"Then how do you know which tree I mean, when I tell you 'from the ceibo'?" I asked.

"Oh, there are 25 locations in Managua that all directions start from," he explained. "This tree is one of the 25." Mary Kay and I looked at one another when I finished translating for her, as if to say, what a crazy way to give directions.

"I should tell you about my first day living at Marta's," I said, as the taxi continued on its trip from the ceibo tree to Marta's house. I moved from the Casa San Juan to the house of Don Fran's daughter Marta in early May. Don Fran thought that her house, located a mile away in the Colonia Centro America, would be easier for me. Living with Marta I could get dinner at night and not have to eat in a restaurant. I was thrilled to be in a family with Marta, her 2-year-old son Marcelo, her teenage maid, Orquidia, and her teenage niece, Carolina.

But on the first day coming home on the bus, someone stole my wallet. A young man who got off with me at Metro Centro tapped me on the shoulder and told me that a man standing behind me on the bus had taken the wallet from the top of my backpack, which I had foolishly worn on my back rather than my front, on the crowded bus. Fortunately, my two cameras, which were packed deeper in the backpack, were untouched. As I stood there at the bus stop, I realized I had no money for the second bus from Metro Centro to Centro America. What am I going to do? I thought, fighting the fear I could feel rising in my stomach. It's my first day at Marta's and I have no idea how to get home.

Standing in the shade of a palm tree at the bus stop I thought, maybe I should walk. I started walking south, not knowing if I was on the street that would take me to Centro America. It was very hot as I made my way from palm tree to palm tree, along the sidewalk of the busy Carretera Masaya highway, hugging each tree to get into its shade.

The sun beat down from directly overhead and the air was beastly hot, even though it was early-May and almost the rainy season. My hair was totally wet as if I had been swimming, and stinging sweat dripped into my eyes and off my nose.

What if I can't find Marta's house? I mumbled to myself aloud in English. All I have is a scrap of paper where Marta wrote 'Del Ceibo, 6 cuadras al sur… ' but where the heck is 'Del Ceibo'? I could feel the desperation rising in my throat as I lunged from tree to tree along the highway, not knowing where I was or where I was going. Nothing looked familiar. Maybe I should go back to Metro Centro and try to find the Casa San Juan, I thought, not knowing what to do next. After standing motionless for 5 minutes, like a statue of a woman glued to the side of a palm tree, I finally turned around and headed back to Metro Centro.

Eventually, as I came closer to Metro Centro and familiar places, in the distance I saw a restaurant where I had eaten dinner several times. After crossing over the wide highway, I walked up the three steps to the entrance and tearfully told a familiar-looking waiter, who was standing by the glass door, "Someone robbed me on the bus, and I don't know how to get home."

The waiter, Eladio, ushered me into the restaurant to a seat by the counter. "Do you want something to drink?" he asked noting the wet hair sticking to my forehead and the sweat dripping off my nose.

"I don't have any money," I whimpered.

"No importa," he said and brought me a glass of lemonade. Eladio took the piece of paper with the address and the phone number so he could call Marta.

She came immediately in her little VW bug to rescue me, very worried because I was by then several hours late.

Mary Kay just looked at me in horror and said nothing about my tale, glad our taxi driver had brought us safely home to Marta's house.. She and I knew that if Katie's temperature did not rise again, the baby would be released from the hospital the next morning, and we could bring her home as my foster child.

Gail picked us up at Marta's house in her red sports car at 6:00 a.m. to go to the hospital. After parking the car in the hospital parking lot, we entered the hospital, greeted the day guard, and climbed up the stairs to the second floor to find Doña Lidia feeding Katie with a syringe full of formula. Mary Kay had brought new clothes and diapers from Omaha for her to wear going home. After Doña Lidia finished feeding the baby, Mary Kay put Katie in a disposable diaper and dressed her in a yellow top with matching bloomers, covered with colorful pictures of tiny animals. She brought baby shoes and tiny yellow socks to the hospital to complete the going-home outfit, but Katie was not happy when Mary Kay tried to put the shoes on her. Katie had worn socks but not shoes in Rolando Carazo, and had worn neither socks nor shoes in the hospital.

"What more do we need to do to get out of here?" Mary Kay asked me.

"I have no idea. Let me ask the head nurse," I replied as I searched for the nurse in charge. I didn't want to just walk out of the hospital with the baby without some sort of permission.

When I finally found the head nurse in the little office just outside the door to the ward, she told me that the baby couldn't leave until the doctor released her, so we sat down to wait for Dr. Karla Fuentes to make an appearance and sign us out. Two days before we had walked out of the hospital accompanied by Dr. Fuentes when we went to the clinic in search of measles vaccine and no one stopped us. But this time three American women would be walking out alone carrying a Nicaraguan baby. We needed papers.

When Dr. Fuentes arrived in the room, she went over what had been done and showed all the medical records to Katie's new mother. Since Mary Kay was also a pediatrician, there were enough Latin terms and medical words that were similar in both languages for them to communicate unaided. Additionally, Dr. Fuentes had been studying English at the UCA, the University of Central America. By using basic English and Latin words, both doctors could understand each other. I just stood around listening, in case anyone needed translation.

Holding the documents that might be needed to get us out of the building, we headed for the door. When we approached the day guard, he greeted us with a big grin and asked, "Going home?"

The day guard, who was named Mario, looked closely at the baby who gave him a big smile. Her face was wide open from the double cleft lip and palate, and her cheek was decorated with a 2" wide piece of tape holding securely to her face the feeding tube, coming out of her open mouth and nose. "Que linda (how pretty)," he said to her with a big smile, and didn't pull back in shock.

Perhaps he has seen a baby like this before, I thought, especially since many cleft lip and palate children in Nicaragua do not receive surgery until they are older, if at all.

I had seen Mario every day for 10 days, and he knew how worried I was before Mary Kay arrived. He seemed intrigued to see an American woman acting like all the Nicaraguan mothers with sick babies. And now that Katie was better, he rejoiced with us, not knowing the difficulties we still faced to get her legally adopted and out of the country.

Gail took us to Marta's house in the red car. Since there was no crib in the house, I searched for my suitcase which had hard sides and zipped fully open. I put a pillowcase on the bottom, knowing the baby would sleep easily on the hard floor. "This will work," I said, as I positioned it carefully on the floor at the end of my bed so I wouldn't step on her if I got up during the night.

Marta got a rocking chair from the Casa San Juan, so Mary Kay could rock the baby when she held her to feed her with the syringe. Every four hours or so, Katie would cry to be fed, so Mary Kay and I were like parents of a newborn, up and down all night, neither getting enough sleep. Additionally, the heat made sleeping difficult. I had become used to sleeping with an electric fan blowing over me, but Mary Kay remained too hot to be able to sleep, even with a fan blowing directly on her. She dripped with sweat continuously and began to have trouble walking. "Be sure you drink enough water," I warned her. "You are probably sweating as much as you are drinking."

Getting worn out with the heat and the lack of sleep, my anxiety was further heightened with news of various strikes, possible layoffs, and increasing tension with the new government. I hope we can get Katie and Mary Kay out of here before any fighting breaks out, I thought.

The first hurdle we had to jump through was getting approval of the adoption by the adoption consejo (council). We asked the new director of Rolando Carazo to set up a meeting with someone from the adoption consejo, and kept being told, "They will meet with you tomorrow," but it never happened.

"The adoption consejo is never going to agree to meet with us," I told Mary Kay. "They will just keep saying 'tomorrow' until you give up and go home. We have to look for some method to waylay them, or we'll never get the signed permission that the court needs to do the adoption."

We continued to gather other documents we needed to complete the adoption, to get a Nicaraguan passport, and to obtain a U.S. visa for the baby. "I know a photography place to get her passport picture taken," I told Mary Kay. "When I get off the bus at Siete-Sur, it is right there by the bus stop. They are sure to know what size and type of photo is needed for a Nicaraguan passport and perhaps even for a U.S. visa."

We took the bus to the photo shop with the baby dressed in her cutest little pink dress. Katie was not at all pleased to have her picture taken that day, and kept screaming and crying as we tried to calm her enough to sit on her mother's lap and look at the camera.

Finally, the photographer, in desperation, took a picture of her screaming with her cleft deformed mouth wide open. When we returned to the photographer the next day to get the picture he had produced, what we saw was a passport picture that showed a thin, scrawny, wailing baby, with a face that looked destroyed. She looked like a dying waif on a poster for UNICEF.

The photographer was apologetic that the baby looked so miserable in the picture. He offered to take another one if we brought her back. I told him, "No, this one will work," thinking it might not hurt to have a picture that looked like an ad for dying children. I tucked it into my fanny pack for future use while Mary Kay paid the photographer.

We walked up the hill to Rolando Carazo to see if the Director had contacted the adoption consejo about Katie's adoption. She had not, but we found that the adoption consejo was meeting that day at Rolando Carazo in one of the cottages.

"This is good news," I told Mary Kay. "We can look for the head of the consejo and waylay her." We knew that the consejo was meeting in the room just inside the door, so we sat in wait outside, leaning on a small stone wall by the sidewalk in front of the cottage, knowing the members of the consejo would eventually have to take a break.

When the head of the consejo emerged, Mary Kay ran up to her, dropped to her knees on the cement sidewalk, and threw herself at the woman as if to tackle her, grabbing her around her legs, sobbing and crying in a loud voice, "My baby needs to go to the US or she will die! My baby need to go to the U.S. or she will die!"

The elegantly-dressed upper-class Nicaraguan woman, standing immobile in high heels with someone as big as a Nebraska football player wrapped around her knees, looked terrified. Mary Kay was huge compared to most Nicaraguans. And she was on her knees with her arms wrapped tightly around the woman's legs keeping her from moving, bawling loudly and yelling in English. I rushed over, knowing the head of the consejo had no idea what Mary Kay was screaming and quickly translated, "My baby needs to go to the U.S. or she will die."

Leaning over the crumpled heaving body of Mary Kay, still entwined around the woman's legs, I handed the terrified woman the little passport picture from my fanny pack. She evidently had never seen an unrepaired cleft lip and palate, took one look, and screamed, "Dios mio! Dios mio!" (My God! My God!). Mary Kay let go of the woman's legs, and the head of the consejo rushed back into the meeting with the picture.

Helping Mary Kay to her feet, I thought, What have we done? as I fearfully began to assess the situation. But within minutes, the consejo had approved the adoption, and the director came out of the cottage, gingerly keeping her distance from Mary Kay, and brought me Katie's picture and the signed document approving her adoption.

We left quickly to catch the bus, clutching the approval document from the adoption consejo and the passport picture. We had the document we needed for Katie's adoption, but I wondered how this event would affect the upcoming adoptions of Roberto and Erik. Would the consejo ever be willing to deal with me again after all this?

The next day, Suzanne Erickson and Lorraine Spencer arrived from Adoption International, the adoption agency in Omaha, to see the two boys and assess what would be required to complete those adoptions. Gail Wilson, in her red sports car, took me to the airport to get them. I told her, "There may be a lot of stuff. They are bringing water beds for Ana Maria and Bryan, as well as coming to see about the adoption of Roberto and Erik."

Gail Wilson was an interesting person. The first month I was in Nicaragua in 1990, while I was living at the Casa San Juan, a very strange American woman, with a flashy red sports car, came to stay there. Gail was in her late forties and stood about 5'8" tall. Her hair was shoulder length and blond, but with dark roots. After she unpacked and settled into her room, she told me that she was a freelance reporter for several American and European newspapers. She impressively dropped their names, and continued to explain her work. "I write stories about everything that is going on in Nicaragua. I tell them about all the good things the Contras and the other opposition groups are doing here. If the newspaper uses the story, they pay me."

So, that's where the odd stories in English about the Contras come from, I thought. I can't imagine a professional journalist writing the kinds of propaganda-like articles that show up from time to time in U.S. newspapers. Suddenly I realized, Stringers. These stories are written by stringers who are overseas for various personal reasons… like perhaps not being able to keep a job in the U.S.

When I asked Gail how she managed to buy a red sports car in Nicaragua, she told me she had sent it down by ship from Miami, and it had just arrived after two months. Gail loved to tell fantastic tales. "When I entered Nicaragua from Honduras, I had a lot of trouble at the border," she told me, "but I converted the man at Immigration to Christianity and he let me in." Later, another favorite was, "I am sleeping with the Captain of the UN Peacekeepers. He's from Spain you know." There was something about how she acted and talked that made me wonder whether to believe anything she said. Most of her stories seemed odd and unlikely to be true. I could tolerate a little oddness (she had a car, after all), but Don Francisco could not. Gail had lasted at the Casa San Juan only one day before Don Fran asked her to leave. He was concerned she could bother the other guests. After Gail moved, I continued to keep contact with her, visiting her in the house she eventually rented and going with her in her car around Managua. She was more than happy to pick me up and take me wherever I wanted to go. I think she was very lonely.

As Suzanne and Lorraine exited customs, Lorraine looked very upset. The first thing she said to me was, "The water beds were stolen in Guatemala when we changed planes. As we got off the plane, I saw a man take the two boxes off the moving belt and put them in a different pile. When we got here they weren't on this plane." I was heartsick for the two dying children who needed those mattresses so badly.

After filling out a missing luggage form, we drove to Marta's with the luggage that had arrived with them. Gail Wilson seemed delighted to have two more Americans to befriend and offered to come get Suzanne and Lorraine to take them wherever they wanted to go. It struck me that Gail had very little to do. She didn't seem to have a real job. Sometimes she wrote articles, but mostly she liked to hang out with us and tell stories about being a sexual abuse survivor. After a day riding around with Gail in the red sports car, Lorraine asked me quizzically, "Do you believe any of the things she says?"

"Not many," I told her. "I'm fascinated, though, about where she gets her money. That's an expensive car."

As the days wore on, Mary Kay got more and more anxious and less able to cope with the heat. She also appeared to have trouble walking any distance. When I told Lorraine about Mary Kay's troubles, she said, "Oh, Mary Kay has MS, and her muscles get weak in hot water or in the heat of summer."

I was furious! "Why didn't you tell me this?" I demanded.

"You sent her down here to me. If I had known that, I could have found her a place to stay with air conditioning. This heat is going to make her sick… or disabled."

Why didn't anyone tell me this? I wondered. They must have known it was important. It made me wonder if there was anything else about her that they had neglected to tell me.

It wasn't long before Mary Kay, Suzanne, and Lorraine were all sick with diarrhea. Unlike me, they hadn't been in Nicaragua long enough to develop some immunity to the local germs. At the pharmacy, I bought packets of suero, the salt, sugar, and potassium, developed by UNICEF to treat children with diarrhea, and mixed it up for them. "I can't drink this," complained Lorraine. "It tastes like salt water."

"It is salt water," I told her. "It is to replace your electrolytes, which include salt." I continued urging them to drink the concoction I had mixed for them. "Guys," I said, "you will get really sick if your electrolytes get any more out of whack." Still they resisted. "Drink it!" I ordered, remembering how sick Ruth Thone had been in 1984. "Hold your nose and you won't taste it." They hesitated, held their noses, and, in unison, all three drank it down. Within hours they all felt better.

After solving that problem, it was time to solve the next; we needed to get Mary Kay into air conditioning before her MS got worse and required her to use a wheelchair.

"What will I do if she can't walk?" I complained to Lorraine and Suzanne, still angry at them for not telling me everything I needed to know. I remembered that the hotel next to the Casa San Juan had air-conditioning, so Marta called and took Mary Kay and Katie over there in her little VW Bug. In addition to air conditioning, the hotel even had a crib with mosquito netting over the top. No more sleeping on the floor in a suitcase for Katie. Soon after arriving, Mary Kay called us to say how nice and cool it was. "I'm going to sleep well tonight," she said, forgetting that the baby was going to wake up every 3-4 hours to eat, and she was going to have to do all the feedings.

Suzanne and Lorraine visited Erik and Roberto every day all week at Rolando Carazo, chauffeured over and back by Gail in the red sports car. At the end of the week, after meeting with the adoption unit at the central office of Mi Familia, Suzanne and Lorraine flew back to Omaha with information for the two families who were interested in adopting the boys.

A few days after they left, the headlines in La Prensa, in oversized large black letters read, "LLEGO INVIERNO" (winter arrived). The rainy season, which Nicaraguans call winter, was upon us. I thought surely they must be kidding. It was 90 degrees, but Marta insisted we were in winter. "This is the hottest winter I've ever experienced," I told her, laughing at the incongruity. Winter in Nicaragua, I thought. What a joke.

Unbeknownst to me, when the first rains come, the termite eggs that have lain dormant during the dry season hatch all at once and cover the walls for about 24 hours with baby termites. Shortly after the bugs appeared on our wall and Marta had explained to me what they were, I got a hysterical phone call from Mary Kay screaming, "Bugs! Bugs! Thousands of bugs."

I tried to explain that they were baby termites and wouldn't bite. More importantly, they would disappear in 24 hours. She was not at all reassured and told me she had covered Katie's crib with a blanket. "Don't do that. You are going to smother her," I advised. But she had already contacted the desk, and as we talked, I could hear the noise in the background of the workers in the process of moving her to a different room, that didn't have a termite hatchery.

May Kay wasn't used to getting up during the night to feed a baby. Not getting enough sleep, the heat, plus super high anxiety had pushed her to the breaking point. "Let me take Katie tonight so you can get a full night's sleep," I offered. When she agreed, Marta and I brought Katie home in Marta's little car, and I put the princess back into the suitcase on the floor at the foot of my bed.

About 4 a.m. Katie woke crying to be fed. I picked her up and realized she had pulled the feeding tube out of her stomach. About 12 inches of rubber tubing flapped around in the air, still taped to her cheek. I looked out the window into the darkness. "There is no way I can call Mary Kay at this hour," I realized. "I'm going to have to put this tube back down, or Katie will be screaming with hunger until daybreak".

I can do it... I know I can... I saw Mary Kay demonstrate it to the residents. "OK kiddo," I said, looking down at Katie, who was now calm, silent, and wide awake.. "We are going to have to put this in ourselves. Your mother is across the city. Now you need to help me by crying." Mary Kay had told me that if a baby was crying, the tube couldn't go into her lungs, because the epiglottis closes when babies cry.

Would Katie cry? Of course not. I poked the back of her throat with the end of the tube and she smiled broadly and laughed. She knew me. This was a game… "Cry Katie, cry!" I begged as I kept poking the back of her throat with the tube. All I got were more wide smiles. "Do you know what time it is?" I asked the smiling baby, holding her little head out in front of me in my left hand. "It is not play time. It's 4:00 a.m.!" She smiled at the words and giggled. "Come on, cry for me… please," I begged as I poked the back of her throat with the end of the feeding tube yet again. "I don't want this to go into your lungs." Finally, Katie, sick of me poking her, began to cry a little. I immediately popped the tube down in one quick motion, hoping to God it wasn't in her lungs. "Let's check for bubbles," I said as I put her down in the suitcase on the floor to go get a glass of water. No bubbles formed when I put the other end of the tube in the water. The tube was in her stomach. "OK, We're good. I'm going to feed you now," I promised, as I picked her up and held her like a football in my left arm, taking her with me to the kitchen to get the formula from the refrigerator to warm up so I could fill the syringe.

The next day, Eduardo Carson, the Canadian special education teacher who worked at Rolando Carazo, suggested an attorney he knew, an older woman, Miriam del Socorro Quezada, who had been in the department of social services during the Sandinista government. She knew how the adoption process worked in Nicaragua, so we contacted her.

There was no original birth certificate for Katie, or rather, for Eliadora Moreno. Although we knew the baby had been born in Leon, Senora Quezada, the attorney whom Eduardo referred to as Doña Miriam, said it would be faster to get an original birth certificate issued if we said she was born in Managua. Doña Miriam obtained an original birth certificate with Managua listed as Eliadora's place of birth. With the birth certificate in her original name and the approval from the adoption consejo in hand, the attorney just had to find a judge who would do the adoption, which wouldn't be an easy task.

Things were heating up between the new government and public employees. Managua was on edge, and judges were threatening to go out on strike. Trouble was coming—you could feel it. You could almost taste it. We needed to move fast to get this adoption done before everyone went out on strike or fighting began.

Mary Kay, Katie, Doña Miriam, and I went to the courthouse in a taxi to search for a judge willing to do the adoption.

"Sit toward the middle," I told Mary Kay as we entered the taxi. "Sometimes the doors on these old Lata cars from Bulgaria fly open when the taxi driver turns a sharp corner.

I saw a woman fall out of one the week before you came. Fortunately, she landed on her feet and held onto the open door and remained upright."

"Life here is always an adventure, isn't it?" commented Mary Kay sarcastically as she struggled to get into the taxi, while I held the baby for her.

As we walked along the corridor of a plain looking public building, which on the inside looked more like a school than a courthouse, we spotted the open door of a courtroom where a judge had just finished performing a wedding. As soon as the couple came out into the corridor, Doña Miriam, with us in hot pursuit, barged into the courtroom. "Can you do this adoption?" our attorney begged. "The baby's sick. She needs to go to the US." The judge looked at Katie's deformed face and agreed.

Watching all the activity occurring at the end of their wedding ceremony, the newly married couple wandered back into the courtroom and asked if they too could stick around for the adoption. Mary Kay invited them to come sit with us in the courtroom, and we all sat watching the judge go over all the documents our attorney had prepared plus the document from the adoption consejo giving permission for the adoption to take place. All the documents were in order according to the judge, so he signed the appropriate papers, and Kathryn Elizabeth Moreno Bowen became legal. Little did I know that this would be the first of 18 adoptions I would facilitate for special needs Nicaraguan children.

Before she could get a visa to enter the US, Katie needed a new birth certificate and a Nicaraguan passport in her new name, a medical exam by a physician approved by the U.S. Embassy, and four photos with the left ear showing for the visa. Doña Miriam applied for the Nicaraguan passport using Katie's new birth certificate that she had obtained from the government by showing the adoption certificate.

But Doña Miriam could not get the U.S. Visa. That is something a U.S. citizen needs to do. So, after getting the new birth certificate and Nicaraguan passport, Mary Kay, Gail, and the baby went off together in the red car to the Consulate attached to the U.S. Embassy, leaving me fretting that Gail would say or do something at the Consulate to screw up this adoption and perhaps the adoption of Roberto and Erik. But they were successful in getting the packet that identified the documents needed for a U.S. adoption visa.

The photographer knew what was required for a quarter turn U.S. visa photo with the left ear showing. Katie was more cooperative this time and her official visa photo didn't make her look like a baby in need of child protective services.

They drove around the Plaza España neighborhood of Managua, looking for a Nicaraguan doctor's clinic attached to his house, and eventually found one of the three doctors approved by the U.S. Embassy to do the medical exam needed for the U.S. Visa.

He looked the baby over, signed the medical form, attached a picture, and sealed them in a manila envelope.

Once Mary Kay got all the documents that were needed, they all went back to the U.S. Consulate to obtain the visa, apparently the first adoption visa issued since the U.S. Consulate opened for business after the Sandinistas were defeated and Doña Violeta was inaugurated as president in April 1990.

The next day, Gail drove Mary Kay, Katie, and me to the airport for their flight to the U.S. Watching the plane roll down the runway, Gail and I breathed a huge sigh of relief when we saw the wheels lift off the ground. "Go! Go! Get out of here," I yelled. "This country feels like it's going to explode."

# Chapter 11

# Snow White

After getting 5-month-old Katie and her mother safely on the Continental Airlines flight to Miami, Gail and I drove to the Rolando Carazo Children's Center where I had not been with the children since Katie was hospitalized, nearly a month before. As Gail and I entered the infirmary, Zaidy greeted us with the news that there was a beautiful new abandoned baby in the infirmary. She had come into Rolando Carazo while we were travelling around Managua, trying to get the documents needed to whisk Katie out of the country before the city exploded in violence.

Zaidy was right. The baby was gorgeous! Catia was 9 months old, tiny, probably only 10-12 pounds, with jet black hair that grew in ringlets around her beautiful face, covering much of the chalky white skin that indicated serious anemia. When she saw us hanging over her crib, her face lit up in a beautiful smile. I was smitten and immediately named her Blanca Nieve (Snow White). Clearly baby Catia was bright and alert, despite being malnourished. Each day when I went to the Center, no matter how hard I tried to get her to suck or to swallow the life-saving liquid, Catia would not drink the milk I offered. She would push the nipple out of her mouth and let the milk run down her chin.

"Come on, baby, you need this stuff," I begged. But she wouldn't take it. Without thinking, I instinctively looked around for a feeding tube like Mary Kay and I had been using to feed

Katie. I knew how to insert a tube into a baby's stomach. I can do this, I thought. Or at least Zaidy can. This baby needs milk, It was clear, if we hoped to save her, we desperately needed a feeding tube to get fluid into Catia's stomach.

Suddenly I realized that all the feeding tubes had gone to Nebraska with Katie, neatly packed in the suitcase sitting under her mother's seat on an airplane, now flying high over the Gulf. There are no feeding tubes here in the orphanage or in the hospital, or anywhere I know in the entire country, I remembered. Why didn't I think to ask Mary Kay to leave a few of them, in case we needed them for another baby? Why?... Why?... How could I have been so stupid? I raged, as I saw beautiful baby Catia shrinking before my eyes.

Each day I tried every hour or so to feed her, but Catia would take none of the formula or even the water I offered. On my last day at Rolando Carazo before I left for home, I went to see my Snow White to try again to feed her and say good-bye.

As she came into my outstretched arms, ringlets of black hair remained on the sheet, and handfuls of her hair continued to fall, like black falling rain. I froze in horror. Holding her tight against my chest, I yelled at Zaidy, "We are losing her. We are losing her... for lack of a feeding tube!"

As I held Catia tightly to my chest, I couldn't breathe or move . Fear washed over me in waves. Rocking back and forth, hugging her I sobbed, "I am so sorry, Catia... We can't save you... We didn't keep the feeding tubes... Please don't die..." as my tears fell like Baptismal water on her now bare head cradled against my chest. My Blanca Nieve died of malnutrition and dehydration the week after I left Nicaragua.

By June of 1990, the new government of President Violeta Barrios de Chamorro, or Doña Violeta as everyone called her, had been in office less than two months, but already was having serious problems. On the one side she was pressured by the World Bank and the International Monetary Fund to reduce the number of public employees, and on the other side, she was pressured by the unions aligned with the Sandinista Party to protect public service jobs.

The newly elected vice-president, Virgilio Godoy, a founder of the PLI (Independent Liberal Party), one of the center-right parties that aligned to create the 14-party effort called Union Nacional Oposicion (National Opposition Union or UNO), attempted a coup against the President, with a small militia force of armed men.

Doña Violeta would not permit him to take over the presidency, and called for the Army to protect her government. Staying loyal to the President, the Army disarmed the dissidents loyal to Vice-President Godoy, herded them onto Army trucks, and deposited them miles outside of Managua on land owned by the Cardinal.

The Army officer in charge told the members of the militia which had attempted the coup, "You can walk home from here," and left them stranded to figure out how to find their way home.

That evening, Doña Violeta went on TV and announced, "There is only one army of Nicaragua, and it is the Sandinista Army," which was then the name of Nicaragua's Armed Forces. The general in charge of the army at that time was Ex-President Daniel Ortega's brother, Humberto. He had stayed loyal to the newly elected president and did not attempt to overthrow her, despite fears that he might do so in favor of returning his brother to power.

President Violeta Barrios de Chamorro stated to the TV audience, "General Humberto Ortega is a professional soldier."

Standing beside her in the TV studio, General Ortega stated, "Doña Violeta Barrios de Chamorro is the elected President of Nicaragua, and I am sworn to uphold her government."

It was an amazing moment to watch. She trusted him and kept him on as General of the Army, despite pressure from the far right to replace him. He reciprocated and remained loyal to her and prevented the country from descending into chaos.

Perhaps democracy can work here, I thought, still wondering why no one was arrested for the coup attempt, and why Virgilio Godoy remained as Vice-President. I definitely don't understand Nicaraguan politics, I realized, shaking my head.

Despite the election of Doña Violeta in February 1990, which brought the Contra War to an end, there were lots of guns in Nicaragua. The Contra Army, which had caused so much bloodshed in the 1980s, was no longer supported by the U.S. government in 1990, but the fighters were still heavily armed. As the Contra Army was dismantled and soldiers were discharged and headed home from the front, they kept their weapons with them. Also, as the Sandinista Army was reduced from 100,000 to 16,000, those soldiers also kept their weapons and brought them home with them after being discharged. Unemployed and armed young men can be a serious problem for any government. Something had to be done.

Immediately after Doña Violeta was inaugurated in April 1990, at her request the United Nations sent in Peacekeepers to help her disarm the country. Suddenly, everywhere you looked there were young soldiers wearing bright blue berets. In Spanish, Peacekeepers are called the Cascos Azules, the 'Blue Helmets,' but they wore blue berets, not helmets. The Peacekeepers appeared young, perhaps 19 or 20 years old, with the short hair of army recruits and the skinny arms and legs of youth. They were dressed in khaki uniforms with United Nations insignia on their shoulders and arms, but did not carry weapons. They travelled around Nicaragua in UN-marked dark blue pick-up trucks. They resembled Boy Scouts on a camping trip, hanging over the side of the pick-ups, waving at passersby. While the Peacekeepers came from all over the world, if a Peacekeeper spoke English, you could count on hearing an Irish brogue, since Ireland provided the United Nations with many Peacekeepers.

The officer in charge, a Colonel from Spain, was taller, heavier, better built, and older than the young men in their blue berets. While he looked like he could be their Boy Scout leader, he also exuded a professional military aura of 'no nonsense.' For those of us who lived in Nicaragua at the time, it was very reassuring to see the young men with their bright blue berets riding around in U.N. pickups, everywhere we looked.

The Cascos Azules had their hands full collecting the tens of thousands of weapons that existed in varying states of disrepair. Many of the guns were already broken and of little use, but if the gun were functional, the peacekeepers broke it into pieces to disable it. All the broken pieces of armaments were then dropped into deep pits and burned. I am sure some functioning weapons were not turned in and were buried in the back yard for future use. But little by little, workable guns disappeared from Nicaragua, and the violence dissipated. Killings after the Peacekeepers arrived involved mainly disputes about land, when people who had fled Nicaragua after 1979, attempted to recover their land, which had been given to others during the land-reform era of the 1980s.

As public employees learned of the government's plan to fire about half of them, demonstrations bubbled up in Managua and all over the country. A bit oblivious to the rising tensions among public employees, over the July 4th weekend a group of us English speaking internationals decided to go to Matagalpa to visit the Association of Farmers and Ranchers and view some of their projects.

I was so looking forward to the trip; I had not been out of Managua since arriving in April, because of the situation with Katie. In fact, I had not even been able to see my son graduate from Harvard's Kennedy School, because the week of the graduation, Mary Kay and I were at the hospital helping Katie get the milk out of her lungs.

Matagalpa is high, cool, and hilly. It felt good to get away from the stifling heat, the flatness, the trash, and the noise of Managua. Walking on the streets of Matagalpa reminded me of walking around the Cornell campus in Ithaca. Everything was uphill, in Matagalpa even more so. It was hard to believe I was in the same country as Managua.

Immediately after arriving in Matagalpa we visited the grave of Ben Linder, one of the two US citizens killed by the Contras; the other was a nun who had lived in Nicaragua for years. Linder worked as an engineer purifying water from a river near Matagalpa. But when not working, he performed as a clown and rode a unicycle to amuse the children. He exuded both idealism and competency. One day when he was repairing a pump by the side of the river, a Contra snuck up behind him and shot him in the head.

His parents flew to Nicaragua to attend his funeral and bring his body home. But the community begged his parents to allow him to be buried in the "local" section of the city cemetery of Matagalpa, the highest honor they could give him. His parents agreed to leave him buried in the place and among the people he loved so much.

Subsequently the Casa Ben Linder was created in Managua where US internationalists gather for lectures in English and to meet other Americans who are working in Nicaragua. Leon opened a Café Ben Linder on the corner across from the main building of the university, UNAN-Leon. The rear wall was totally covered by a large mural of Ben on his unicycle with the children playing around him. The café served sandwiches and drinks and had a cybercafé attached. In the past, the café also had a little art gallery where they hung paintings done by disabled Nicaraguan artists. Unfortunately, the Café Ben Linder closed in 2006 and was replaced by a bank. But recently it has reopened again as a café. The mural is still there.

In Matagalpa, for the first time, I saw coffee growing. Look at how short these coffee trees are. I thought coffee grew on big trees. These are little more than 6-foot-tall bushes. The coffee beans growing on them were green because it was early July; they would not turn red until harvest time in November.

I also saw fields and fields of corn and dry beans growing together—double cropping—along the sides of steep mountainous slopes. I was excited to photograph the beans growing on the slopes to show to my husband, Dermot. I had seen pictures of him in Columbia looking like a mountain goat, hanging off the side of a steep hill, examining the bean experiments at CIAT (Centro Internacional Agricultura Tropical). I was sure he'd be interested in mountain-grown beans in Nicaragua. He'll want to see this double-cropping, I thought, as I ventured out to photograph the beans growing up the corn stalks.

One of the farmers, Enrique Soza, had just returned from a two-day workshop put on by the Association of Farmers and Ranchers. "They taught us how to make compost and how to grow crops without using store-bought fertilizer," he explained. "It will save us money on fertilizers and be better for the land." Now it was his job to teach the other farmers in the area the technique.

We walked all over the field, up and down hills, in between plants. There was not a square inch of level land. The plants looked like they were hanging onto the earth for dear life. Enrique Soza was highly amused... and confused. "Why is the Señora kneeling down taking pictures of the plants?" he inquired of one of the other women in our group. Quizzically he kept staring at me on my hands and knees, trying not to roll backwards down the steep hill, taking close-up photos of the bean plants.

Someone finally explained to him, "Her husband studies beans, and she is looking for signs of disease in the plants." As I photographed bean plants tangling their way up the corn stalks, I realized the plants looked healthy and without disease, not even insect damage! The beans were thriving, twisting their way up the corn stalks, which makes it hard to harvest them by machine, but no matter—no machine was going to go up and down those hills! The corn and beans would be harvested together by hand.

We stayed at the Matagalpa Inn, where there was no running water. Someone had put a large metal oil drum full of clean rainwater in the bathroom in a corner of the shower. The trick was to not contaminate the clean water in the oil drum with soap or dirt.

To flush the toilet, you had to scoop out a gallon or so of water from the oil drum with the bucket located nearby and dump it into the toilet. Taking a shower required standing near the drum, reaching over the edge with the blue plastic cereal bowl that sat on the metal cover, scooping some water with the bowl and pouring it over your head, being careful all the time to not get dirt or soap into the clean water in the drum. Fortunately, I had had the experience of flushing and showering like this at Marta's when we had our no-water days.

We returned to Managua on Sunday to find the city in turmoil. In our absence, the students at the Jesuit University, the University of Central America (UCA), had demonstrated against the government and its proposed cutbacks in jobs. They burned tires and marched around singing revolutionary songs. Unfortunately, a policeman shot and killed one of the students on Saturday. Sunday the students marched around the streets of Managua carrying his coffin on their shoulders, before they brought it to the cemetery for burial. By the time we arrived back Sunday afternoon, the air was filled with the smell of burning tires. The threat of a general strike hung over the city like a pall. Something was going to happen; you could feel it; you could hear it; you could smell it.

Early the next morning before 5 a.m., I heard a strange noise in the dark. Someone was banging on the metal grate of the window in the living room of Marta's house where I was staying. Clang, clang, clang, wake up! I crept out of my bedroom and over to the window on my hands and knees, peeked out, and saw it was the man from next door, Luis Contreras.

"Do you have any oil?" he demanded. "I need some. The Army is coming to take over our houses, so they can shoot demonstrators as they march along the Carretera Masaya. Lend me some oil. I need to oil my gun."

Luis Contreras was about 35 years old, 5'6" tall, with dark brown skin and tightly curled short black hair. He had fought as a Sandinista against Somoza in the Revolution in 1979. By 1990 though, he had lost his physically-fit-soldier physique, and now looked overweight and a bit clumsy. He also appeared to have a drinking problem, the few times I saw him outside in the cul-de-sac in front of our houses with his wife and three young children, including a newborn baby girl.

The drainage ditch at the end of our dead-end street was all that separated us from the Carretera Masaya. From the porch, we had a clear view of the highway, a straight shot. All day and all night large trucks rumbled by, carrying produce from the countryside into the Managua markets to feed a city of over a million inhabitants.

High on each truck, one or two women sat on top of mountains of onions and other produce, their colorful many-pocketed aprons flapping in the breeze.

Beside them, turned upside down, were the large woven baskets they would fill with vegetables and balance on their heads, when the truck finally reached the market.

"The Army is coming. They are going to shoot demonstrators from our porch. Give me some oil," Luis Contreras demanded again.

I gave him some cooking oil through the metal grate covering the window, entered Marta's bedroom, and woke her saying, "Luis Contreras, the neighbor man, thinks the Army is coming to commandeer our houses. I think he's drunk. Why would the Army take over our houses to shoot at demonstrators marching along the Masaya highway?"

Marta, still half asleep, got up saying, "I'll talk to him."

I left Marta's bedroom and turned to look out the window just as the sky showed the first pink rays of daylight. In the dim light, I could see Luis standing on our porch in full battle gear, a bandolier of bullets draped over his right shoulder and another over his left. In his hands, he clutched an AK-47.

"Dios Mio," Marta cried out when she saw him through the window. "I am taking Marcelo and going to my father's house."

"No you're not," I ordered, trying to take charge of the situation. "You're staying right here. It is too dangerous near the UCA. Listen to the noise… those are bombs going off in the distance. It's coming from the UCA, near the Casa San Juan. You are not taking that baby out in the dark into a riot," I yelled loudly, suddenly remembering all the Spanish words I needed.

"I am going to my father's!" she yelled back.

"We are safer here than in the Casa San Juan with your father," I explained more quietly. Marta by this time was shaking with fright.

She had lived through the fighting of the Revolution, which toppled the dictator Anastacio Somoza eleven years before. Post-Traumatic Stress Disorder, I thought, as I looked at her in front of me, shaking like a leaf.

The noise of our argument woke Orquidia, Marta's maid, and her niece Carolina, both 16 years old, a little young to remember much about the Revolution. When they saw Marta shaking, however, they also became frightened.

"What is going on?" Carolina demanded. Orquidia said nothing, but went directly to get her machete. I had seen her wield it the week before when she cut some limbs from the mango tree above our roof. You wouldn't want to be on the receiving end of that thing in her hands, I thought.

I quickly realized that I was the only grown-up in the house that was thinking clearly, while two were standing paralyzed, shaking like leaves and one was girding for battle with a machete. I began issuing directions. "If any shooting starts, we go into Marta's bedroom; it has thick walls, no windows, and a wooden door." They looked at me blankly. "We have plenty of water saved in the large Pepsi bottles," I assured them, "and we have a barrel full of water in the bathroom. We're fine! We just need to stay here in the house and not panic."

Outside was eerily quiet. The usually heavily travelled Carretera Masaya was silent… no sounds of trucks whizzing by. No trucks rushing into the city carrying fruit and vegetables for the day to be carried in huge rattan baskets on women's heads.

As daylight increased, out the living room window I could see trucks filled with vegetables and upside down baskets sitting dead still on the highway, women perched on top of them quietly waiting… for something.

As I turned around to go get dressed, I heard the first shots! Rat-a-tat-tat! Rat-a-tat-tat!

"Get Down," I screamed in English to the girls and hit the deck, crawling on my belly like a Marine around rocking chairs towards Marta's bedroom. The girls followed suit. Soon we were all sitting on Marta's bed, wooden bedroom door shut tight, hearing gunfire outside our front door. What in God's name is Luis shooting at? I thought. All I had seen on the highway were farmers with their trucks and peasant women sitting patiently on top of the vegetables. Dear God, I hope he is not shooting at them.

Then, I heard what sounded like incoming shots bouncing off the outside wall of the house and figured he might have been hit. In English I muttered to no one in particular, "If you are stupid enough to start this, you can bleed to death on our front porch for all I care. I am not going out there to save you." Then I tried to say in Spanish, "Boys and their toys!" It didn't translate well.

"What Anita? What?" cried Marta, almost hysterical and trying to make sense out of my 'boys and their toys' comment. Cynicism and idioms don't translate well, especially not when you are under incoming fire and your listener borders on complete hysteria. Soon the shooting stopped, and I assessed our injuries.

When I hit the deck, the St. Christopher medal Theresa had given me for protection bounced up and hit me in the teeth. Orquidia hit her knee on the rocking chair when she dove for the floor. Carolina emerged unscathed, and Marta was not physically injured, but she continued to tremble uncontrollably. Marcelo slept through it all.

I gingerly slunk out of the bedroom and peeked out the living room window expecting to see Luis dead on the porch, his two bandoliers of bullets still draped across his chest and his AK-47 close by. But he wasn't there. And there was no blood. Strange, I thought. Slowly I opened the front door and crept outside on my hands and knees to look for bullet holes in the wall by the front door, but there were no signs of gunfire. When I scooted back into the house, no one was there. They had all disappeared completely out the back door, I was the only one left. Oh, Great! They are supposed to be taking care of me, and they've all run away.

All morning I stayed alone in the house wondering where they had gone and worrying if they were safe. Finally, about 11 a.m., Marta excitedly called me by phone from the Casa San Juan, her father's hotel. "Anita, you should take your camera and go outside," she said. "There are barricades, for the first time in 11 years."

No word about why she had abandoned me. No word about where the 16-year-old girls were. No word about Marcelo, although I was sure she had taken her two-year-old son with her. Nothing about the morning, just "go take some photos," as if we had all been enjoying a nice July summer day together... instead of hiding from flying bullets at daybreak.

This is crazy. I wonder if I will ever get used to this culture? I pondered. Grabbing my cameras, I went across the drainage ditch and up onto the Carretera Masaya, the major highway into Managua from the south, still clogged with giant trucks full of vegetables and women with their baskets. I think I understand them, and then I don't. There must be cultural differences I don't fully understand. A lot of times I just can't predict what they are going to do.

In Nicaragua, all the main roads are paved with a form of cement paving stone that is about 12" square, but all four corners of the stone are carved out, so that another equally shaped paving stone can be laid beside it. They all fit together like a cement jig saw puzzle, but with pieces the same shape and size. It is said that the dictator, President Somoza, owned the cement factory and required that all roads in Nicaragua be built with these cement-block paving stones. In truth, they make very good roads, despite the inherent corruption involved. Students had dug up the cement paving stones from the highway and piled them into barricades on all four sides of nearly every intersection in Managua.

All the barricades I could see stood about four feet high and stretched across the entire highway or the entire cross street, blocking all traffic. The barricade across the Carretera Masaya on the north side of the intersection was basically a pile of paving stones placed piggly-wiggly on top of one another. But the barricade on the east side of the intersection was a work of art. Those students had exactly arranged each paving stone, so they formed a beautiful pattern.

They must be architecture students, I thought. Or else they suffer from a bit of obsessive compulsive disorder.

People from the neighborhood were milling around admiring the architectural students' work when who should arrive? The ice cream man! I burst out laughing. It reminded me of his arrival, marching in line behind the angels, during the solemn Good Friday procession of Holy Week. Whenever two or more are gathered in My Name, there will be the ice cream man, I reminded myself giggling. He never failed to appear whenever there was a crowd. I often wondered where the ice cream men hid out with their little refrigerated push carts, so they could pop out whenever they spotted a group.

A day that had started out with gunfire was now turning, by lunch. into a block party. No one could go anywhere because of the barricaded roads; busses and taxis were not running; nothing was moving in a city of over a million people. The general strike was on. No one went to work because no one could.

Somehow, Marta, Marcelo, Carolina, and Orquidia got back home late in the afternoon in Marta's little car. I tried to figure out how they got around the barricades. The students must have let them pass, I assumed.

Many people in Nicaragua did not have refrigerators in 1990, so food was sure to become scarce very quickly. Fortunately, Marta had a refrigerator, so we had enough to eat.

Anticipating trouble weeks before, we had also planned for a water shortage, filling dozens of plastic two-liter Pepsi bottles for drinking and cooking, and filling the large drum in the bathroom for flushing and bathing while we still had water coming out of the taps. But, the house next door, owned by Luis Contreras, still alive and uninjured despite his war games episode of the early morning, quickly ran out of water, since no water was flowing out of any faucets in Managua during the general strike.

The next day, after we noticed Luis' wife trying to strain the muddy water which had flowed off their roof into a rain barrel, Marta told me, "They have a very small baby in that house, and she needs clean water. Let's see if we can go get some water for them."

So off we went in Marta's little Volkswagen bug, driving on sidewalks and around barricades at each intersection, to get water from the swimming pool at her sister Carmen's house nearby. As we approached each intersection, Marta yelled out the window at the students manning the barricade, "We are going for water for a baby." They waved us on and let us drive around the barricade and up on the sidewalk.

When we got to Carmen's house, there was a large above-ground swimming pool made from heavy plastic, containing gallons and gallons of water. We filled five one-gallon jugs and a large covered plastic tub with water, all the empty containers we could find to bring with us to collect water.

We put them in the backseat to bring to the Contreras family to boil and use for the baby, but as we were leaving Carmen's backyard, Don Francisco called on Marta's cell phone. A group of four British businessmen and their wives had arrived at the Casa San Juan the day before the general strike, and had planned to leave that morning in their rented 12-passenger van for an exploratory trip around Nicaragua, looking for business opportunities to invest in, as well as enjoying the beauty of Nicaragua's lakes and volcanos. Now, they were going nowhere… and the Casa San Juan didn't have food to feed them.

Marta and I decided to try to get food at the Roberto Huembe's Market about a mile away. We drove through people's yards, convincing students manning the barricades that we were after food. Fortunately, the students weren't adversarial, and let us drive around them.

None of the stalls were open at Huembe's. It was locked up tight. I had ordered a gold cross for Katie's baptism in August, but the jewelry store was locked up as tight as the vegetable stalls. Looking at the locked up stores and stalls, Marta remarked, "In the final two weeks of the insurrection in July 1979, the population got so hungry they broke into the supermarkets and stripped the shelves bare." Huembe's wasn't going to let that happen again.

Later, as we drove around the large parking lot in front of Huembe's, we spotted a man standing under a tree on the side of the road with several fish in a basket beside him on the ground. He was willing to sell us three fish for an astronomical price.

Marta bought them to bring to the Casa San Juan to feed the British guests. Finally, we headed home, around barricades and over sidewalks and lawns, with water for the baby next door.

That afternoon, as we were watching TV, the picture went blank, but we could still hear the audio. Students had broken into the television studio and were yelling and scuffling with TV employees, as they took over control of the station. Then everything went quiet. The TV station was off the air.

Rumors began to spread that the U.S. was going to invade to stop the general strike. I told Marta, "I doubt it. Most people in the U.S. don't even know where Nicaragua is. The U.S. government certainly doesn't care about a general strike in Nicaragua."

By chance, Dermot called that night checking on my travel plans home. He had not heard that Nicaragua was in the middle of a general strike. The idea that the rumors floating around that the US would bomb or invade stuck him as ludicrous. That made me feel better, but just to be safe I told him to call Brian in Washington. "Ask him to tell someone there not to bomb Managua," I begged. Clearly, with all the stress, I was losing my mind, imagining all the bad things that could possibly happen, no matter how illogical. "I don't know if my flight to Mexico will go when scheduled," I told him. "The Managua Airport is still closed, and my flight is supposed to leave in two days."

The barricades began to come down when the government agreed to pay workers a lump sum of $2,000 if they would voluntarily leave government service. They could not apply again for a government job for 3 years. No one would be fired. The reduction in public employment, required by the International Monetary Fund and the World Bank, would come about through buyout and attrition.

The night before my scheduled flight, there was word that the airport might open the next morning. Marta called a taxi driver she knew, Cristhiam Hernandez, and convinced him, after much arguing and wheedling, to pick me up before dawn, even though he was very reluctant to drive in the dark. We scooted up on sidewalks, on lawns and around the holes in the pavement where the paving stones used to be. No one was manning the barricades any longer. The airport was open. My flight would go on time, the first flight out of Managua after the general strike.

As we took off for Mexico City, with the wheels lifting off the ground of the tiny airport and the plane surging upward, the pilot tipped a wing toward the perfectly shaped Volcan Momotombo, belching smoke and volcanic ash over Lago Xolotlán. I whispered, like General McArthur when he left the Philippines, "I will return." But right then, I had had more than enough of Nicaragua for a while. I wanted to go home.

# ACKNOWLEDGEMENTS

Many thanks to Professors Todd Robinson, Lisa J. Knopp, and John T. Price, of the University of Nebraska Omaha's Creative Non-Fiction concentration , for welcoming me into five of their classes and encouraging me to "make scenes come alive for the readers." For the students in those classes who took the time to read and critique my attempts, especially Philip Froese, Shawnelle Alley, and Maritza Estrada, and for Professor Joan Latchaw, who supervised Philip as he edited part of the manuscript for his senior English project, I am eternally grateful. Without their thoughtful critiques and confused looks at jargon and sentences that didn't make sense, this story would not have been completed. Special thanks to Dr. Jane Juffer of Cornell University and my long-time friend Shirley Maly who read and critiqued the final manuscript in its entirety.

# AUTHOR BIO

Ann Coyne, PhD. is Professor Emerita of the Grace Abbott School of Social Work at the University of Nebraska Omaha, where she taught for 43 years. In 1990, while doing a sabbatical in an orphanage in Nicaragua, she began looking for adoptive families in Nicaragua and in the U.S. for Nicaraguan disabled children Over 20 years, she was able to find homes for 18 disabled Nicaraguan children. In 1994, she developed a sister university relationship between the University of Nebraska Omaha and the National Autonomous University of Nicaragua-Leon and took students there annually for 24 years. Additionally she assisted various departments at UNAN-Leon by accompanying UNO English, Special Education, and Social Work professors to teach graduate courses there for faculty and by bringing UNAN-Leon English professors to Omaha for intensive English classes. She developed a social work master's degree at UNAN-Leon, since none existed at any other university in Nicaragua. She brought U.S. social work professors to Leon every other month for two years to teach intensive graduate courses, until Nicaraguan professors were able to obtain master's degrees and take over teaching the courses. Utilizing her Rotary connections in Omaha and in Nicaragua, she was involved in developing a maternal and child health care center in Managua, a school for deaf children in Leon, and building houses for 72 families in Leon after Hurricane Mitch.

In 2002, Dr. Coyne was awarded the international "Service Above Self Award" from Rotary International and in 2011 was awarded the "National Lifetime Achievement Award" by the National Association of Social Workers. She currently lives at Kendal at Ithaca, a retirement community in Ithaca, NY.

Made in the USA
Middletown, DE
23 September 2024